Coping With Your Pain and Suffering

Encouragement When You're Not Healed But You Love God

Matthew Robert Payne

Coping With Your Pain and Suffering

Copyright © 2015 by Matthew Robert Payne. All rights reserved.

No part of this publication may be reproduced, stored in a retrieval system or transmitted in any way by any means, electronic, mechanical, photocopy, recording or otherwise without the prior permission of the author except as provided by USA copyright law.

More information about Matthew can be found at
http://www.matthewrobertpayneministries.net

Matthew also can be found on Facebook in a group that he runs called "Open Heavens and Intimacy with Jesus." that can be found here
https://www.facebook.com/groups/OpenHeavensGroup/

Matthew has written several other books before this one and they can be found on his Amazon author page here

http://www.amazon.com/Matthew-Robert-Payne/e/B008N9R896/ref=ntt_athr_dp_pel_1

Scripture quotations marked (NLT) are taken from the Holy Bible, New Living Translation, copyright © 1996, 2004, 2007 by Tyndale House Foundation. Used by permission of Tyndale House Publishers, Inc., Carol Stream, Illinois 60188. All rights reserved.

"Scripture taken from the New King James Version. Copyright © 1982 by Thomas Nelson, Inc. Used by permission. All rights reserved."

Editor Melanie Cardano from www.upwork.com

The opinions expressed by the author are not necessarily those of Revival Waves of Glory Books & Publishing.

Revival Waves of Glory Books & Publishing
PO Box 596
Litchfield, IL 62056
United States of America
www.revivalwavesofgloryministries.com

Revival Waves of Glory Books & Publishing is committed to excellence in the publishing industry.

Published in the United States of America

Ebook: 978-3-9592-6722-9

Paperback: 978-1-365-76024-2

Hardcover: 978-1-943847-67-9

Acknowledgments.

Melanie Cardano

I want to thank Melanie for going through this book and making it better through her copy editing and proofreading. Melanie has become a fan of mine and enjoys reading what I write. She is the best editor that you can get. Melanie can be hired through www.upwork.com.

Bill Vincent

I want to thank Bill from Revival Waves of Glory Books and Publishing for publishing this book of mine.

My Mother

I want to thank my mother, June Payne, for all the time she spent with this book and all the love and support that she has given me throughout my life. She really is the best mother you could have.

My Father

I want to thank my father, Bob Payne, for loving me, supporting me, and giving me time with my mother. Only you know how much you have given for my sake.

Jesus Christ

I want to thank you for always being my friend though all of my life. You are my joy, my reason to live, and my hero!

Dedications

I dedicate this book to all the people who are suffering right now and can see no hope in the immediate future for recovery. It is my prayer that this simple book ministers to you.

I dedicate this book also to Petra my friend who has given me a donation large enough this month to get the cover designed for this book. If you like the book and the cover pray for Petra who suffers terribly. God knows who you are praying for.

And lastly, I dedicate this book to Cathy, whose new kitten story is in the second last chapter. It was with her in mind that I wrote everything in this book.

Table of Contents

Acknowledgments. 3

Dedications 4

Introduction 7

Chapter 1 Pain is a Part of Life 8

Chapter 2 Tribulation is Part of Life 18

Chapter 3 The Agenda of Satan 36

Chapter 4 The Agenda of God 47

Chapter 5 Have I Done Something Wrong to Deserve This? 54

Chapter 6 Is This My Destiny? 65

Chapter 7 Am I a New Testament Job? 74

Chapter 8 Finding Joy in the Journey 83

Chapter 9 Some Impossible Cases in the Bible 94

Chapter 10 Can an Unhealed Person Bring God Glory? ... 113

Chapter 11 Can Others be Blessed by Me? 123

Chapter 12 What Was Paul's Thorn in the Flesh? 130

Chapter 13 Does God Love Me Less Than Others? 142

Chapter 14 How Do I Get the Faith to be Healed? 149

Chapter 15 I Am Loved Without Cause 158

Chapter 16 Heaven Will Be Glorious 164

I'd Love to Hear from You! 169

How to Sponsor a Book Project 170

Other Books by Matthew Robert Payne 171

Introduction

I copied this from the end of the book but it makes good little introduction

If you are reading this book, I want to start by saying God loves you.

I love you, too. Yes, God has done a new thing in my life as I have written this book and I knew He would. But I wrote this book for all the hurting people who will either buy it or download it. I really want to encourage you to look to Jesus and be reassured of His deep love for you. Your life is precious to Him and He wants you to live it to the full.

Though you may feel insignificant or weak, I want you to know that you have much potential and God has a great purpose for you in life. If I could somehow stop your suffering and pain, you know that I would. In the meantime, I send you my love and spiritually hold hands with you and bless you.

I wrote this book to encourage you that you are loved despite the fact that you are suffering with pain or sickness. I envisage when I am healed one day, that I will have another book of answers to follow this book. It is my prayer that this book ministers to your spirit.

Chapter 1
Pain is a Part of Life

It doesn't matter where you live in this world, you will discover that pain and suffering are part and parcel of life. Since Adam disobeyed God, these consequences of sin have made their presence known in the whole world. You may live in a village in Africa, or in an apartment in the Upper West Side of New York, it will not make a difference because pain and suffering became an integral part of the human experience way back in the Garden of Eden.

I am not a trained theologian or a professional communicator, I write simply because I love the Lord Jesus Christ with all my heart. I just want to share my current level of Biblical understanding with others, in the hopes that I may be able to help my reader in some way. Like every Christian, I realize that I am on a spiritual journey where God is in the process of changing my theology and other views, from where I was, to where He wants me to be. I'm not there yet, but at least, by the grace of God, I am on my way.

When I choose a subject for a book, the Holy Spirit drops the title for it into my spirit and then, He gives me the chapter titles. Though I feel my writing is led by the Holy Spirit, I know that God will continually take me to new levels of understanding. However, if I wait till all this becomes a personal reality, then perhaps, I may be too feeble to write, or too old to even remember what I know.

As the title suggests, this book is to address the reality of pain and suffering. I have had personal experience in these things and it's my desire that my words and the Scriptures I use, as well as my personal stories, can bring comfort to people. I want to encourage my readers that even though they may be experiencing pain and suffering, they are deeply loved by God just as much as any healthy or rich person is loved by Him.

Christ came to break down all earthly divisions whether by class, cultural, or otherwise. The impartial God shows to all people the same love, grace, blessings, and benefits of His salvation, *"for there is no partiality with God"* and *"God shows personal favoritism to no man." Romans 2:11, Galatians 2:6.*

There are many ways that we can suffer and some people who teach on healing can be quite hurtful in the way that they sometimes express their faith. I pray that this book will tread the middle ground, brings comfort and edification and a sense of worthiness to those who are not yet healed or free of their personal suffering.

King David had this to say: *"The troubles of my heart have enlarged; bring me out of my distresses! Look on my affliction and my pain, and forgive all my sins. Consider my enemies, for they are many; and they hate me with cruel hatred." Psalm 25:17-19.*

The Book of Psalms, although loved by many people for its poetry and worship, can in my opinion, be a very sad book to read. The verse above is just one of many where we see David desperately calling out for God to help him.

David, whilst still a young lad, was personally selected by God's Prophet, Samuel, to rule God's chosen people, yet David's life was certainly not an easy one. His personal suffering wasn't really sickness or illness, but emotional and spiritual pain, which can often be more debilitating than physical pain. To me, David's suffering and his cries to God seems to be an ongoing theme in the Book of Psalms.

However, all through other parts of the Old Testament, God sings the praises of David as being one of His most righteous kings who ever reigned. God highly honored David, yet this much loved man was not free of personal pain and suffering. Many people could see this as being an enigma or contradiction.

Personally, I have suffered with a combination of Bipolar Disorder and Schizophrenia for close to twenty years. In the midst of my suffering, I tend to avoid reading this Old Testament Book simply because of David's constant pleas for help in his suffering. To a Manic Depressive, (Bipolar) like myself, I find some parts of David's writing just too depressing.

Still, people like David, who have suffered greatly and yet have endured and overcome, are just so inspiring to me. David really suffered much, yet he lived in the presence of

God even in that sad state. David is a hero of mine, not so much for his worship songs, though I love all the songs that are composed from his writings, but because he was a righteous king totally devoted to the same God that I am in love with today.

David was an Old Testament saint who was refreshingly honest about his own feelings. When he was angry, he let God know it! When he was sad and crying on his pillow all night, he not only let God know it, but as a writer, he recorded it for all of us - who have spent a night in tears. I suspect that David would have been one of the most honest and transparent people in his day.

Through the course of this book, I want to be absolutely transparent to my reader. With that transparency, I hope through my stories that you, too, will feel encouraged that a man of God can be honest and disclose things that are not often preached about in today's pulpits.

The Apostle Paul in the New Testament suffered a lot. Some of his trials and sufferings came from the hand of God, while others obviously came direct from Satan, using other people. In the following verse, Paul talks about the type of trials and sufferings that came from the hand of God. These trials are to fashion and train us to be obedient children.

"For they (i.e. earthly fathers) *indeed for a few days chastened us as seemed best to them, but He* (Our Heavenly Father's chastisement) *for our profit, that we may be partakers of His holiness. Now no chastening seems to be joyful for the present,*

but painful; nevertheless, afterward it yields the peaceable fruit of righteousness to those who have been trained by it." Hebrews 12: 10-12.

We, like Paul, are to recognize that God chastises His children for our profit: that we can be partakers of His Holiness. There is a false understanding going around these days that as Christians, we don't need to suffer. There are Christians who teach that you only suffer if you have a wrong doctrine: or if you don't believe the right things, or you are not wearing your spiritual armor. There are all kinds of popular teachings these days that appeal to certain people. For example: most Christians in the West will very strongly argue that there is a pre-tribulation rapture of the church, and I believe this is because they do not want to endure any personal suffering that has been prophesied as coming in the End Times.

I know that I have been personally chastised by the Lord. I have suffered and I have been purified by the Lord and I am extremely grateful for it. So, too, was Paul. He went so far as to say that an undisciplined child could even be an illegitimate child. *"But if you are without chastening, of which all have become partakers, then you are illegitimate and not sons." Hebrews 12:8.*

As Christians, this is a wake-up call! Father God disciplines those whom He loves. Paul warns us that chastening does not seem joyful at the time, but instead, it is painful. However, our suffering can lead to good wholesome fruit. A wise farmer knows when and how to prune his trees to produce quality fruit even though the tree itself may not appreciate his efforts. There are whole groups of Christian parents or "do-gooders" who don't preach on such verses. They refuse to bring chastisement onto their little darlings and their children ultimately grow up to be anything but "darlings" in society.

Now, of course, Paul wasn't a man who habitually gave in to his fleshly appetites. No, Paul was continually conscious of having to deliberately put to death any of his carnal desires. Why? Paul wanted more than anything else to become the man that God wanted him to be.

Paul knew that God's training through discipline would produce both inner peace and righteousness. His desire to bring others into the Kingdom caused Paul to be totally honest about his inner thoughts, so that thousands of years later, we can still relate to him today.

Some people say Paul struggled with his new identity in Christ. These people will argue that he never reached a place where Christ was so alive in him, that his flesh was fully crucified and subdued by the Holy Spirit. To my mind, this is an error. Except for our Lord Jesus, Paul was one of the most righteous and holy persons to walk this earth. Yet, this holy man of God gave a chilling testimony of personal suffering: Let's look at his vast suffering resume:

"From the Jews five times I received forty stripes minus one. Three times I was beaten with rods; once I was stoned; three times I was ship-wrecked; a night and a day I have been in the deep; in

journeys often, in perils of waters, in perils of robbers, in perils of my own countrymen, in perils of the Gentiles, in perils in the city, in perils in the wilderness, in perils in the sea, in perils among false brethren; in weariness and toil, in sleeplessness often, in hunger and thirst, in fasting often, in cold and nakedness." 2 Corinthians 11:23-27.

And so, if Paul was beaten with rods and was often whipped, and if he was homeless and out in the cold with no food or shelter, who do we really think we are that we won't experience some form of suffering as well?

Paul is a man to be greatly admired. Although much of his writings are still too profound for me to fully understand, the following verse is what he had to say about suffering: *"I consider that the sufferings of this present time are not worthy to be compared with the glory which shall be revealed in us. For the earnest expectation of the creation eagerly waits for the revealing of the sons of God."* Romans 8:18-19.

It's important to realize that God's glory will not be revealed to us, but "in us." Therefore, we don't need more faith, more power, or more anointing - *we simply need to use more of what we have already received!* In the above Scripture, Paul used the words "earnest expectation" which means: "intense anticipation" – Paul, by the inspiration of the Holy Spirit, says that the whole of creation is waiting for us *to manifest what is already in us.*

Paul suffered greatly as a follower of Jesus. More than once, he was given 39 lashes. More than once, he was stoned.

More than once, he was beaten with rods so all his bones were bruised, which according to medics today would have caused him agony for about six weeks. Paul had a super-hard time of it, yet the average Christian in the West doesn't know anything about real suffering for the Gospel. Today, as I write, the Christians in northern part of Iraq are certainly suffering greatly. In fact, many believers all around the world, in darker countries, have been continually suffering for the sake of Christ.

If you are personally suffering and are in pain, rest assured that many have gone before you and have suffered as well. You can be assured that the same gracious and loving Father in Heaven, who loved Paul and David and yet allowed them to suffer, loves you too. Though we may not fully understand why we suffer, we can be all sure of one thing, God has never changed. We have His promise on this in Malachi 3:6 *"For I am the Lord, I do not change."*

Perhaps, you don't physically suffer with illness. Perhaps, you have had your spirit broken and it seems beyond repair. If King David was still alive, he would have understood you because he knew all about a broken heart that doesn't want to go on living. King Solomon, who was the wisest king of Israel, spoke about the devastating hopelessness that comes from a broken spirit: *"The spirit of a man will sustain him in sickness, but who can bear a broken spirit?" Proverbs 18:14.*

Do you have a broken heart? Is your pain unbearable?

Four times in my life, I have had God sovereignly send someone to have a talk with me when I was suicidal. On all four occasions, I had decided to kill myself and I knew exactly how to do it. On each of those occasions, it was what these people said to me that turned me around.

One time, I was on the way to have a few beers and then catch a taxi out to a certain bridge to throw myself off it. A total stranger, who just happened to be a pastor, prophesied to me on the street. This man told me that God knew I was on my way to have a few beers, for I planned to catch a taxi to this particular bridge and to jump off. He asked me if he could pray for me and prophesy further over me.

I was both stunned and very emotional that God would do this for me. The words he spoke back then, twenty years ago, have sustained me through years of some horrible sufferings due to mental illness, spiritual and emotional pain.

One day, a man came to this world and He healed every person who came to him to be healed.

"And Jesus went about all Galilee, teaching in their synagogues, preaching the gospel of the kingdom, and healing all kinds of sickness and all kinds of disease among the people. Then His fame went throughout all Syria; and they brought to Him all sick people who were afflicted with various diseases and torments, and those who were demon-possessed, epileptics, and paralytics; and He healed them." Matthew 4: 23-24.

Jesus was a wonderfully gifted healer. He was so full of compassion for all who were afflicted. In his three year ministry period, He must have laid hands on tens of thousands and healed them all. The truth is: if this same Jesus was on earth today in the flesh and He came to minister in a conference in your city and you went forward in faith to be healed by Him, He *would* heal you.

I cry as I write this because I so long to be healed! I suffer mostly because I still carry much unhealed emotional pain from my past. I would really love my crying to stop. I feel that this book is not only going to be encouraging for you to read, but it will actually be cathartic for me to write.

The Bible is such a source of encouragement. However, even if we never have the faith to heal ourselves, or we never meet a gifted healer who can heal us, we can look forward to a future day when we can live in an earth described below by the Apostle John. I know that I certainly look forward to that awesome day.

"And I heard a loud voice from heaven saying, "Behold, the tabernacle of God is with men, and He will dwell with them, and they shall be His people. God Himself will be with them and be their God. And God will wipe away every tear from their eyes; there shall be no more death, nor sorrow, nor crying. There shall be no more pain, for the former things have passed away. Then He who sat on the throne said, "Behold, I make all things new." And He said to me "Write, for these words are true and faithful." Revelation 21:3-5.

Chapter 2
Tribulation is Part of Life

Almost since the beginning of time, people have gone through all manner of tribulations. However, an ongoing trial of tribulation could seriously wear a person down. These people who were once vibrant and fresh, would begin to feel like they were soiled, broken, discarded, or overlooked by many others. Like a freshly picked flower wilts and dries up, our faith could easily dry up to the point that we could even be ready to give up on God.

My testimony: At the age of eight I received Jesus as my personal Savior. This happened when a children's evangelist told us kids that we could have a special friend who would talk to us and never leave us. I lived with a father who was quite angry at times, but from eight to fourteen, my young faith flourished. Then, when I was fourteen, I was molested by a man in his thirties on a deserted beach. Having your sex drive activated by a man at that age is not a good start for any youth.

Soon, I was going back to the beach for the wrong sort of attention. My singing praises to Jesus started to wilt at church. Feeling unloved and not understood, I set my path to a life of sin that would haunt me and put me under a feeling of condemnation for many years.

My secret sin drew me away from Jesus and into a sad life of hiding the real me. I was confused and I was feeling dirty inside, but in a sad way, I felt loved by the attentions of other men. What started as sexual abuse actually led to a life of sin and debauchery!

The Israelites had a promising start, first through the loins of Abraham, and later through the twelve tribes descending from Jacob. Joseph, the second youngest son of Jacob, through a series of traumatic events, had become second in charge to the Egyptian Pharaoh. He ultimately saved the Jewish people from starvation and their numbers increased rapidly.

However, their increased numbers eventually became a threat to the leadership of Egypt, so the children of God were actually forced into slavery. From being God's chosen people, they had become a persecuted race! In the fullness of time, by an amazing way, God used Moses to miraculously save them from the Egyptian's oppression. Nevertheless, years later, they were not satisfied with God as their great King. Instead, God's called-out ones wanted to be just like the pagan nations surrounding them. They wanted a physical king to rule over them.

Therefore, God, through the prophet Samuel, said to His people: *"Thus says the Lord God of Israel: 'I brought up Israel out of Egypt, and delivered you from the hand of the Egyptians and from the hand of all kingdoms and from those who oppressed you. But you have today rejected your God, who Himself saved you from all your adversities and your tribulations; and you have said to Him, 'No, set a king over us!' Now therefore, present yourselves before the Lord by your tribes and by your clans. And when Samuel had caused all the tribes of Israel to come near, the tribe of Benjamin was chosen." 1 Samuel 10: 18-19.*

The Israelites had become so complacent about God's goodness that they were no longer thankful for all His supernatural interventions to keep them safe. The Lord had performed so many mighty works for them, yet this faithful God was no longer honored. Their rejection of Him was evidenced by their desire to be like the heathen nations surrounding them.

Sometimes, we as Christians can be so attracted to the things of the world that we can forget about the goodness of God that we have experienced. Instead of being grateful for His grace, love and mercy, we can find ourselves wanting to chase after things of the world. We forget that the world only offers temporary pleasures that appeal to our flesh, but God wants us to be motivated by His eternal treasures that bring the truly honorable things into our life.

God did not interfere with man's free-will choice back then and He certainly will never interfere with our free-will choice today. This is because God the Father paid the ultimate sacrifice for man's free-will choices. Father God sent His one and only beloved Son to the cross to carry in His Own body all the collective wrong choices of mankind.

God had been rejected by His Own people, so He gave them what they wanted. A tall and well-built handsome man named Saul was finally chosen to be king. He came from the tribe of Benjamin, not from the tribe of Judah that David had come from.

My Bible notes say, "That the tribe, clan, family and son were determined probably by casting lots. What Samuel had done by privately anointing Saul in 1 Samuel 10:1, was publicly confirmed so that both the people and Saul would have assurance of God's choice." However, in 1 Samuel 15:22-23, King Saul defiantly disobeyed God's prophet, therefore Samuel was led by God to anoint David from the line of Judah, to rule as king after Saul.

In the meantime, Saul's demonic jealousy of young David caused him to aggressively pursue him for many years. In Saul's obsessive hate and rage, he wanted to kill David. Over the years, Saul's intense hatred and jealousy caused David enormous distress and tribulation.

One day, David quietly snuck up on Saul whilst he was sleeping on the ground with his men. He quietly stole Saul's spear and a jug of water that was next to Saul as he slept. When David and his men departed, they made some noise which woke Saul from his sleep. Later, David told Saul that on that day, he had the perfect opportunity to kill him but he didn't do it. David knew that he was to be the next in line. He knew that because he had shown honor to God's present anointed king, the Lord would deliver him from his tribulations.

David said to Saul: *"May the Lord repay every man for his righteousness and his faithfulness; for the Lord delivered you into my hand today, but I would not stretch out my hand against the Lord's anointed. And indeed, as your life was valued much this day in my eyes, so let my life be valued much in the eyes of the Lord, and let Him deliver me out of all tribulation.*

Then Saul said to David, 'May you be blessed, my son David! You shall both do great things and also still prevail.' So David went on his way, and Saul returned to his place." Samuel 10: 18-19.

When David eventually became king, he reigned for forty years, but his tribulations continued. He had an adulterous affair from which an illegitimate child was born, but later died. His people tried to stone him once, his son slept with one his wives and one of his sons tried to overthrow him. David had enemies all through his kingdom, which saw him penning so many sad psalms that I have spoken about.

I think that to believe that you can live a life free of tribulations is wishful thinking. Preaching that the Christian life can be free of struggle is not only wrong theology, but it can lead people to even more disappointment! Knowing that everyone will experience struggles and suffering actually helps when you are suffering. When I have personally felt drained and overwhelmed within, I have discovered that hearing about others who suffer and yet still persevere, is uplifting news that encourages me to do likewise.

Tribulations didn't just exist in the Old Testament. Jesus spoke of tribulations in the Christian's life as well. Jesus had been teaching on the Parable of the Sower, which according to Him is the most important parable to understand. This parable teaches that we should not only hear the Word of God, but let its truths sink down into our heart so as to establish a strong deep root system that will sustain and protect us from being deceived. He said:

"But he who received the seed on stony places, this is he who hears the word and immediately receives it with joy; yet he has no root in himself, but endures only for a while. For when tribulation or persecution arises because of the word, immediately he stumbles. Matthew 13:20-21.

In nature, a strong root structure is vital for a healthy seed to grow to its full potential. This is also true when God's spiritual seeds are planted in our heart. God wants us to nurture all His precious seeds by meditating on them over and over, thus allowing a strong root structure to develop deep within us. When we take the necessary time and effort to allow God's Word to form deep roots in our heart, we can be sure that no demon or anyone else will be able to uproot His Word from our heart.

For example: we could easily pull up a young 20cm palm tree, but if we waited until the palm plant was say, 80cm high, we wouldn't be able to pull it up with our hands. We would actually need to dig deep around it because of its strong, deep root structure. Palm trees have exceptionally strong root structures.

God wants His children to be strong so that when tribulation or persecution comes, we will be spiritually victorious. In fact, we can even grow stronger than what we would have been before tribulation came. Just one of God's "seeds" can destroy any attack from the devil if we just keep it in our heart and let it dominate us!

Jesus knew that whenever the Word of God is preached, a demonic power may come and try to destroy the good work that it will do in our life. Not only do baby Christians come under attack, but mature Christians as well. We are to be conscious that whenever the Word is preached, these spiritual evil beings will try and defuse any new revelation, by any way they can. They can cause trials and tribulation to dominate our mind, so that the new revelation does not take root in our heart. The bottom line is: if the Christian life did not have tribulation in it, Jesus would not have spoken about it.

In no way am I saying that sickness and suffering is God's will for us, for when Jesus came across people who were sick and were suffering from it, He healed all of them! It is never God's will for us to be sick. Because evil exists in the world, I strongly believe that in this life, there will be tribulation and both pain and suffering can be part of that tribulation.

People like me who suffer are very much aware that Jesus heals today and that healing is part of the salvation package. I would love to walk free of my mental illness, and yet, while I suffer, I take exception to people saying that I don't have enough faith. I guess what I lack is a deeper knowledge and understanding of my new birthrights as a child of God.

Years ago, in all recorded history, not one person had run the mile in under four minutes. Then one day, Roger Bannister broke this record. Athletes, who had previously thought that it was not possible, were suddenly confronted with the fact that it was indeed possible because Roger proved it.

Think about it, in all athletic history, no one had ever run that fast, but since the once impossible became possible: athletes had a brand new mindset when running the mile.

This is also true when it comes to sickness - Christians need to have a new mindset. First, they need to know that it's possible to be healed. Second, they need to know that they are worthy to be healed and thirdly, they need to know absolutely that its God's desire for them to be healed. Otherwise, we will unconsciously go on believing that healing is only possible for the fortunate few. This is where I currently am!

I'm stuck! I know that healing was included in my salvation package. I know that God loves to heal. I know that some people are healed of my condition and have lived totally free of medication ever since their miraculous healing. It's just that at this present time, way down deep in my heart, I still don't personally feel worthy of that healing. I am actually allowing my emotions to overrule the Word of

God! I say this because in my mind, I know that my salvation did not depend on my worthiness or righteousness because the Bible teaches that salvation is the result of faith in Christ's worthiness and His righteousness.

It seems to me that somehow, my faith falters through the distance between my brain and my heart, and you may be experiencing the same problem. The answer, of course, is that God wants us to let His Word and His Holy Spirit have the final say!

Maybe, I do need more personal faith than what I presently have. Faith comes by hearing the word of God according to Romans 10:17. I need to get into the Word more and to meditate more on what God has said about healing. I need God's personal revelation knowledge about His will for me to be set free. Yes, I believe that I have faith for so many things, but at this stage, I do not have enough faith when it comes to healing. I need to seriously pray for new revelation.

As I honestly share my heart with you, I know that I will be touched by the Holy Spirit as he leads me through the chapters he has asked me to write. The Christian life is a continual personal journey of discovery with many bends and distractions along the way for us to negotiate. Praise God, He has not left us alone! He is with us every step of our life's journey.

In the meantime, our Christian life will have tribulation. Jesus reassures every believer to focus our constant attention on Him and His plan for us, so that we are not put off track by any present negative circumstances.

"Indeed the hour is coming, yes, has now come, that you will be scattered, each to his own, and will leave Me alone. And yet I am not alone, because the Father is with Me. These things I have spoken to you, that in Me you may have peace. In the world you will have tribulation; but be of good cheer, I have overcome the world." John 16: 32-33.

Christians are called to identify with Jesus. He knows hard times will exist for us. Hard times create strong character and we need to be strong in God to be His witnesses. Life on earth for Jesus was not easy – He was constantly misunderstood; He was lonely and a man of sorrows just as it had been prophesied in Isaiah Chapter 53. Jesus could have recited this whole chapter long before He accepted His Father's earthly assignment as - *He is the Word of God!*

People see Jesus as someone who had all the answers and that's true, but He was rejected, maligned and mistreated long before the cross. For thirty-three years, Jesus purposely put aside His God nature and as the Son of Man, He had to continually rest in God, His Father. He had to receive His peace and his reassurance from talking to His Father. Jesus had an extremely hard life, harder than Paul's, harder than David's and yet, Jesus learned to live in resurrection power even before He was bodily resurrected.

Jesus modelled life and suffering for us – He didn't just suffer for six hours one Friday. His life was very painful and He is still the most misunderstood Person today.

Many people unconsciously use His name as a swear word, they have no idea "Who" He really is and what He had to suffer on earth. Two billion people may call Him Lord, but few really know Him and understand what He went through growing up and in ministry outside the writings in the Bible. Few people know Him well enough to hear Him tell them about His life on earth and teach them how to follow Him.

Jesus told us to be of good cheer. He overcame the world system and all its temptations. Yet, few people know how to personally overcome these things in their daily experience. There are people who have actually been healed by Jesus, but they still lack a deep and abiding relationship with their Healer.

Then, there are others who remain sick and are still suffering in pain. However, some of these people who still struggle with sickness have been driven so deep into the abiding love of Jesus that peace and joy bubble in their spirit.

I read a book on faith once, where it gave about twenty short testimonies of people who were known by the world to have shown great faith. The first four accounts had the authors confess that the greatest reason for their strong faith was overcoming the trials that they once had in their life. Sickness can be a major trial for anyone to experience, but sometimes, sickness can be the catalyst to thrust a person into a very deep relationship and love for Jesus.

What I am saying is that these people realized that their character had been shaped by God for the good, by *how* they personally dealt with their specific trials.

"And when they (Paul and Barnabas) *had preached the gospel to that city and made many disciples, they returned to Lystra, Iconium, and Antioch, strengthening the souls of the disciples, exhorting them to continue in the faith, and saying, 'We must through many tribulations enter the kingdom of God.'" So when they had appointed elders in every church, and prayed with fasting, they commended them to the Lord in whom they had believed."* Acts 14: 21-23.

Paul says we get a grip on the Kingdom of God through tribulations. Is your life free of trials and tribulations? Are you experiencing a hard or a comfortable life? Is there nothing that you are suffering with? How are you entering the Kingdom? Swimming upstream is hard.

I know that some people who read this book will be far smarter than I am: who are more knowledgeable on healing than I am, and who are more eloquent with words. My desire is to comfort others who suffer like me. I am not writing to impress theologians; I am trying to speak up for those who are currently coping with much pain and suffering in their life.

If that is you, then I pray that you will stay with me. At this stage, I don't know what is coming in my next chapters;

I don't know if you'll understand all that I will try to communicate; and I don't know if you'll agree with everything I write. However, at the end of this book, it is my prayer that you will be feeling better and more loved, not just by a fellow pilgrim, but more importantly, by the One who gave His very life for you.

Paul says that tribulations can really do us good: *'Therefore, having been justified by faith, we have peace with God through our Lord Jesus Christ, through whom also we have access by faith into this grace in which we stand, and rejoice in hope of the glory of God. And not only that, but we also glory in tribulations, knowing that tribulation produces perseverance; and perseverance, character; and character, hope." Romans 5:1-4.*

Yes, Jesus prophesied that we would encounter tribulation in the world and later, Paul explains that through tribulation, wonderful godly characteristics can develop in our own character. Therefore, maybe those who have endured tribulations and sufferings are on the fast track to a better character!

Let's look at some words that we find in the Bible relating to suffering and bring some clarification to them.

- Healing: Some people glibly quote the words *"By His stripes I am healed"* and that is true - see Isaiah 53:5 and 1 Peter 2:24. However, saying these words is worthless to you - if you refuse to believe that all your sicknesses were actually born by Christ on the cross. (I feel somehow that I am talking to myself here.)

- Affliction: *"Many are the afflictions of the righteous but the Lord delivers them out of them all." Psalm 34:19.* The word "affliction" means trials, hardships, persecutions or even temptations. These suffering are things we need to pray for and overcome. We are not "healed" of them! This is confirmed in James 5:13 *"Is any among you afflicted? Let the afflicted one pray."*

- God's chastisement: The word "chasten" comes from a Greek word which means instruct, train, discipline, teach or educate. This word has absolutely nothing to do with sickness, disease, or infirmity. (No responsible parent would punish their own child with these things.) Satan is the author of sickness, disease and infirmity!

We read in 1 Peter 5:10 - *"But may the God of all grace, who called us to his eternal glory by Christ Jesus, after you have suffered a while, perfect, establish, strengthen, and settle you."* God allowed Jesus to suffer in order to fully identify with us. Because of sin in the world, God knew that believers would not be exempt from suffering.

Therefore, it's possible to suffer other than by sickness. It was because Paul could say that he had suffered for Christ's sake that he could say: *"Finally, there is laid up for me the crown of righteousness, which the Lord, the righteous Judge, will give to me on that Day, and not to me only, but also to all who have loved His appearing"* 2 Timothy 4:8.

What did Paul's suffering consist of? It included *"affliction"* as in Psalm 34:19, quoted earlier. *"Chastisement"*

Paul referred to in 2 Corinthians 6:9 and many other hardships listed in 2 Corinthians 11:23-27.

It is very important to note that Paul never referred to sickness or disease as part of his sufferings.

Actually, the disciples rejoiced that they had been beaten, because they felt that they had been counted worthy to suffer shame for Jesus' name. They knew that their only crime had been preaching the Gospel and healing the sick in Jesus' name. *"So they departed from the presence of the council, rejoicing that they were counted worthy to suffer shame for His name."Acts5:41.*

Jesus healed all who were sick because it is His will for all of us to be healed. Our loving Father would never give us sickness to develop our character. Satan gives us sickness because he wants to hurt us and make us feel useless in the Kingdom of God.

"I am the Lord who heals you." Exodus 15:26. What God says is true! God's desire for all of us to be well must be preached, so that faith can be developed. Physical healing is for all who believe! Any form of doubt on our part destroys faith. *"But without faith it is impossible to please Him, for he who comes to God must believe that He is, and that He is a rewarder of those who diligently seek Him."* Hebrews 11:6.

"God is not a man that He should lie, nor a son of man, that He should repent. Has He said, and will He not do? Or has He spoken, and will He not make it good?" Numbers 23:19.

Can God be trusted? Of course, you say. Then, that is Biblical faith. Faith and confession always go together. This is true of salvation and it is also true of healing. How did Paul say we are to be saved? *"If you **confess with your mouth** the Lord Jesus and **believe in your heart** that God raised Him from the dead, you will be saved. For with the heart one believes unto righteousness, and with the mouth, confession made unto salvation." Romans 10:9-10* (Emphasis mine.)

I believe that God is telling us to confess with our mouth God's desire to heal us and believe in our heart that we will be healed and it will come to pass. For His Word tells us that *"Forever, O Lord, Your word is settled in heaven." Psalm 119:89.* Therefore, in God's perfect timing, total healing will "manifest" in my life and in yours.

Some people finish their prayers for the sick with the faith destroying phrase "if it be Your will." Yet, when the outcast leper asked Jesus if it was His will to heal him, Jesus replied *"I am willing: be cleansed"* and he was healed - see Mark 1:40.

Therefore, Jesus has already emphatically told us His will concerning healing. Jesus wants us to know without doubt that God's will today is just the same as it was back then! Scripture confirms this fact in Hebrews 13:8 *"Jesus Christ is the same yesterday, today, and forever."*

Never lose sight of the fact that God is a good God all the time!

Way back in Numbers 21:4-9, we read that some Israelites were complaining about God and Moses, *so the Lord sent fiery serpents to bite them and they died*. When the others repented of their complaining, God had Moses erect a brazen serpent on a pole and all who looked at it were healed. Then, many centuries later, in John 3:14-15, Jesus clearly implied that the serpent typified His being raised upon the Cross. Both our spiritual and physical healing comes from looking to and identifying with Christ crucified, by whose stripes we were healed.

Healing like salvation is by faith in God's word! When we do our small part, God is always faithful to do His big part. God has promised: *My covenant I will not break, nor alter the word that has gone out from my lips." Psalm 89.*

Did Jesus heal everyone? Yes! *"Great multitudes followed Him and He healed them all." Matthew. 12:15b.* This is also confirmed in Matthew 8:16-17 – *"When evening had come, they brought to Him many who were demon-possessed. And He cast out the spirits with a word,* **and healed all who were sick***, that it might be fulfilled which was spoken by Isaiah the prophet, saying 'He Himself took our infirmities and bore our sicknesses'"* (Emphasis mine.)

Whenever Jesus Christ is proclaimed as our sacrifice for sin and sickness, physical healing as well as spiritual salvation will result. Paul must have preached the Gospel of healing because the man who had been lame from birth, heard and by faith, he was healed. (Acts 14:8-10)

I trust that my reader will realize that God not only wants to see everyone saved, but He wants to see everyone saved from all sickness as well.

It's not God's will for any to be either sick or to be lost.

Chapter 3

The Agenda of Satan

I have been taught that Satan was a covering cherub angel of God before pride came into His heart. He was the head angel who had been appointed to lead worship of the Father. Then one day, his gigantic pride and arrogance drove him to the point that he wanted the worship by the heavenly beings and the angels to be focused onto him, instead of unto God.

Ever since that time when Satan and his demonic followers were cast out of Heaven, he has been trying to influence others to follow him. Satan has an agenda, not to save the world, but to lead the world away from God. Satan does not need your worship as a god anymore, for he is happy if you serve 'any' other god, but the one true God. He is happy to do a very effective and deceptive work in the world, with most of its inhabitants doubting his very existence.

In the Old Testament, a false prophet was known by one way: this was to lead the people of God after a false god! If a prophet was found to do have done that, then he was to be stoned.

Satan achieves his agenda on earth by making mankind by in large serve themselves and the lusts of their flesh. He knows that much suffering comes when people act in the flesh. These works have been listed by Paul: *"Now the works of the flesh are evident, which are: adultery, fornication, uncleanness, lewdness, idolatry, sorcery, hatred, contentions, jealousies, outbursts of wrath, selfish ambitions, dissensions, heresies, envy, murders, drunkenness, revelries, and the like; of which I tell you beforehand, just as I also told you in time past, that those who practice such things will not inherit the kingdom of God." Galatians 5:19-21.*

Any of these behaviors or actions will cause one or more people to suffer. Doing any of them is less than God's best for you because they can all cause pain and suffering, yet people willingly choose to engage in them. To those without Christ, the works of the flesh come natural. However, we are to be ever mindful that those "in Christ" who choose to dabble in such activities will give Satan an open door to gain entry into their life. This foothold, once secured, quickly becomes a stronghold, which leads to much pain and misery.

If you have suffered in this life, there could be a chance you have played a part in giving the devil access into your life. For example: the average modern movie has adultery or fornication in it. We watch these movies as entertainment and the world readily accepts the behavior in them as being normal. In the past fifteen years, I think I have only seen three movies that I can remember that actually had a "married" couple make love in the sex scene. Many movies in Hollywood have unmarried couples having sex, or married couples cheating on each other.

In a similar way, we can innocently invite a wrong spirit devil into our homes: popular television dramas have plenty of contentions, jealousies, selfish ambitions, envy, drunkenness and the like in them. We can see things on television today that our grandparents would have been appalled at. Yet, we are told by others that "this sort of behavior is natural and okay because it's just entertainment. After all, to make drama, you need a base of conflict."

Modern producers who are responsible for our television dramas and soapies, along with film producers, choose to use fleshly or carnal things to create drama. My parents recall the fact that sixty years ago, you would never see a married couple in a double bed together, but in two separate beds. Now, there are absolutely no boundaries as to what goes on, or off!

People without the Lord will just naturally go with the flow.

Unbelievers, and sadly, many believers, allow themselves to watch things that their God-given conscience says not to. After a while, they can't even discern what their conscience is telling them, because their standard of behavior has dropped to a lower level. Over time, they hunger for more and more pollution to feed their sin-soaked mind. Paul talks very strongly about this in Romans 1:18-32.

This passage I believe is the key verse – *"Because, although they knew God* (at least by their conscience) *they did not glorify Him as God." nor were thankful, but became futile in their thoughts; and their foolish hearts was darkened." Romans 1:21.*

My Bible notes explain that the word "futile" means: 'To make empty, vain, foolish, useless, confused; the word describes the perverted logic and idolatrous presumption of those who do not honor God or show Him any gratitude for His blessings on humanity."

I remember that pastor and teacher, Andrew Wommack, once said that if we reversed Romans 1:21, *we would become full of God.* He meant that once our heart receives the light of God, we will be thankful to Him and we will glorify God in our life, simply because we will personally know how good He is.

However, in its Biblical form, Romans 1:21 portrays a downward spiral to the pit of hell. Yet, our world today constantly feeds on this very sort of thing. No wonder our society is filled with so much violence, sexual immorality and all manner of ungodliness. Even people of God suffer, because many of them choose to walk in the flesh rather than to walk in the Spirit of God. Not only that, Christians can often suffer terrible abuse, because people of the world do horrible things to them.

The Apostle Peter said: *"God resists the proud, but gives grace to the humble. Therefore humble yourselves under the mighty hand of God, that He may exalt you in due time, casting all your care upon Him, for He cares for you." 1 Peter 5:5b-7.*

Why is casting our cares upon Jesus important? Peter's answer is a warning: "Be *sober, be vigilant; because your adversary the devil walks about like a roaring lion, seeking whom he may devour. Resist him, steadfast in the faith, knowing that the same sufferings are experienced by your brotherhood in the world."* 1 Peter 5:8-9.

So many times, we cast our burden onto Jesus and then, when He doesn't deal with it as fast as we want, we take the problem back and begin to worry again in the flesh. It takes real humility to accept that we cannot deal with our burdens and cares by our own puny strength. To ride the storms of life, we must choose to rest in Jesus; to praise Him and then prayerfully leave our worries in His hands.

Many of us have simply not been taught how to enter into God's rest and how to live in rest. Part of letting go is to be totally convinced in our heart that God is a good God all the time, regardless of circumstances. We must trust in the joy of the Holy Spirit within us to sustain us through trials. (I admit that this is far easier to say than to do.)

Let me be totally honest - it may be okay to lose a job; to lose a wife in divorce; to have a breakdown, but how do you enter into rest when you have suffered with depression and mania for twenty years? How do you keep praising God as your Healer, when God has not healed you? How do you ride through a twenty year storm?

There are no easy answers. All I can say is that I cry a lot and I lift my hands and worship the King who made me, the King who sustains me, the King who visits me in visions, the King who uses me to encourage people, and the King who gives me purpose, as well as many small victories despite my weaknesses.

I am learning to adopt the attitude of Paul and I have begun to glory in my weakness, for when I am weak, I am made strong through the power of the Holy Spirit. Though I have not always seen relief to crippling depression straight away, when I eventually come out of that terrible heaviness, I purposely sit at my computer and write another chapter in my latest book. It's my personal way of getting back at the devil.

You enter God's rest by accepting that in your own strength, you are weak. Through worship and the awareness of God's presence, you can overcome the assaults that Satan throws at you. When depression clouds your joy, wait it out with faith that your joy will return, and always thank God for the good days! Even in the midst of your darkest hours - you can remember the good times you have had with Jesus. Whilst you are down and sad and feeling like ending it all, you look at all your victories, and you muster up strength to fight another day, happy that Jesus knows you and loves you.

It's so hard to praise God as your Healer each week when you don't see that healing manifest, but you continue to watch videos of people getting healed on YouTube and read books about the Biblical truth of healing. You cope, knowing that one day, Jesus might manifest your healing and you will be able to write a song or a testimony for all those who are waiting just like you.

Personally, I have ridden through a twenty year storm by growing each day closer to Jesus and by obeying Him in all I say and do to the best of my ability.

However, the enemy prowls around my life, trying to pull me back into an addiction that I am trying to put behind me. The enemy whispers that God is not fair to me. The enemy throws darts of jealousy that others are invited to preach at my church, because my pastor sees no such ability in me, and that's why I will never become a well-known preacher.

The enemy says I will never be free of sin, because I am lazy, I am too weak and I am a loser. The enemy tells me my dreams of ministry are just delusional, because I will never be free of depression and bipolar. The enemy says that God only hears the prayers of those He loves, but even the prayers of someone like Heidi Baker would never cause Him to heal me.

Yes, the enemy is very much alive and prowls around my life. What is he saying to you? Have you realized that he can't speak the truth? Even a compliment by a person with a demon is flattery, because they are always trying to gain control of those Jesus died for.

However, Jesus said: *"The thief does not come except to steal, and to kill, and to destroy. I have come that they may have life, and that they may have it more abundantly." John 10:10.*

- Steal: The enemy wants to steal our peace, our health, our vision, our dreams, and our purpose in life. Our life can be ruined by him and by others he uses to do his works, *if we let him!* The enemy hates us and he can spew lies at us all day long, but if we know the Word of God and our position "in Christ," we can fight a good battle. But make no mistake, we are in a real battle and that battle intensifies the more we start to live in our destiny.

- Kill: The enemy kills people! If he doesn't kill the body, he wants to kill our vision and dreams by stealing them from us. He will put our dreams to death by having us so worn down by suffering that we simply give up in trying to reach our dreams. He can kill our passion for Jesus if we get carried away with self-pity and a "poor me" syndrome. He will put our fire out! He would snuff our faith completely out if that were possible. He can have us get so angry with God that we may even walk away from intimacy with Him for a time.

- Destroy: There are all sorts of things that he can do to destroy our ministry or our reputation. Satan can have us so run down and so wanting company of the opposite sex that he can tempt us to take what is not ours. He can destroy our name. He can have us fall into an adulterous relationship by telling us that our wife will never understand us the way our new friend does! The enemy can destroy us by enticing us into utter submission to the appetites of our fleshly desires.

Abundance: But Jesus showed us in His teachings and commands how to live an abundant life. His ways will war against our flesh: His ways require the strength and empowering of the Holy Spirit. However, the way of Jesus is a far more fulfilled life. Satan might have a quick fix for us, but we are left with a bad after-taste of shame and condemnation, yet every time we do what Jesus teaches us to do, it leaves us with a satisfied and good feeling and we discover what real life is all about.

Whilst we are in pain and suffering, we can choose to live the most abundant life that we can, or to totally surrender to the devil's lies. It's our choice! We can serve Jesus, or we can serve the world's god. Jesus' brother had this to say about Satan's agenda in many Christian's lives.

"You lust and do not have. You murder and covet and cannot obtain. You fight and war. Yet you do not have because you do not ask. You ask and do not receive, because you ask amiss, that you may spend it on your pleasures. Adulterers and adulteresses! Do you not know that friendship with the world is enmity with God? Whoever therefore wants to be a friend of the world makes himself an enemy of God." James 4: 2-4.

While ever we serve the world and its ways by desiring all that the world offers, we make ourselves an enemy of God. God wants us to love the people of the world and be salt and light to them, but He doesn't want us to be attracted to the ways of the world. We need to stand out as being consistently and pleasantly different to unbelievers.

Satan has many people of faith serving the world, thinking that they can have one foot in the world and one foot in the Kingdom of God. James says being a friend of the world makes us an enemy of God. I have to ask you, how many of God's enemies is He going to allow into heaven?

So what does "serving the world" look like? John, the disciple Jesus loved, gives us some light on this: *"Do not love this world or the things it offers you, for when you love the world, you do not have the love of the Father in you. For the world offers only a craving for physical pleasure, a craving for everything we see, and pride in our achievements and possessions. These are not from the Father, but are from this world. And this world is fading away, along with everything that people crave. But anyone who does what pleases God will live forever." New Living Translation, 1 John 2:15-17.*

Remember always that Satan doesn't need you to serve him, or give him glory, he just wants you to serve any god other than the one true God. His agenda is to have people suffering any way he can. People are suffering all around the world in ways that could be addressed, if the church was reaching out into the community and not just serving their appetites for the things of the flesh.

Many people are suffering in ways that could be fixed with money that you and I have, but sometimes our lust for all that is in the world and sometimes incorrect teaching on giving to the Kingdom, stops us from setting people free of this preventable suffering.

We can in some small way overcome the world and its lusts. Jesus did! *"These things I have spoken to you, that in Me you may have peace. In the world you will have tribulation; but be of good cheer, I have overcome the world." John 16:33.*

Chapter 4
The Agenda of God

Can you imagine being the loving Creator, having dominion over all creation, and yet giving free-will to your created beings made in your image? It would be a highly risky venture, one that could have bad consequences and much heartache. But God did this because He wanted a family of His Own to love Him forever, *simply because they chose to do so!*

Personal choice can be an awesome privilege if it's exercised in wisdom, but unfortunately, this is not always the case. Rather than demanding worship and obedience from us, we have been given the choice to honor and love our Creator as God Almighty, or to love ourselves and promote our own personal desires.

For much the same reason, God had earlier given His angels a free-will. God knew that only those who willingly chose to serve Him would seek and enjoy a relationship with Him. Man speaks eloquently about freedom, but God actually created it.

Well, most of us know the story. Man chose to disobey God and sin entered the world. And from that original sin came all forms of suffering, pain and sickness. It was not

God's intention that man live with any kind of suffering, but it was the dreadful consequence of free will. Since the Garden of Eden, it has still been God's agenda to restore unto Himself a family of His Own to enjoy for all eternity. Therefore, the plan that the triune Godhead had originally agreed on was put into action. His only Son left Heaven and came to earth to redeem man back to His Creator.

"And as Moses lifted up the serpent in the wilderness, even so must the Son of Man be lifted up, that whoever believes in Him should not perish but have eternal life. For God so loved the world that He gave His only begotten Son, that whoever believes in Him should not perish but have everlasting life. For God did not send His Son into the world to condemn the world, but that the world through Him might be saved." John 3:14-17.

It was not just God's intention to save you and me. It's His intention to save the whole world by using us to evangelize in the power of the Holy Spirit with Spirit filled words, signs and wonders. Jesus died to give each of us an opportunity to enjoy a vibrant relationship with Himself and His Father. Through personal belief, in the sacrificial death of Christ and His resurrection, we receive remission of sins and therefore, we enjoy the freedom to walk how God intended and to receive healing, to those who claim it. Jesus became the "firstborn" among many brethren:

"And we know that all things work together for good to those who love God, to those who are the called according to His purpose. For whom He foreknew, He also predestined to be conformed to the image of His Son, that He might be the firstborn among many

brethren. Moreover whom He predestined, these He also called; whom He called, these He also justified; and whom He justified, these He also glorified. Romans 8:28-30.

- Jesus came to be the "first born" of a new breed of humans.

- Jesus came so that we might follow in His footsteps so as to glorify God.

- Jesus came to give His life so that we could become overcoming followers of God.

- Jesus came so that we could enjoy communion with Him and become a blessing to each other and the people of the world that we live among.

- Jesus came that we might be able to overcome the devil: to walk in that freedom of choice and with that choice, walk in wisdom and righteousness.

- Jesus came that the world would have the choice to receive eternal life.

"For the grace of God has been revealed, bringing salvation to all people. And we are instructed to turn from godless living and sinful pleasures. We should live in this evil world with wisdom, righteousness, and devotion to God, while we look forward with hope to that wonderful day when the glory of our great God and Savior, Jesus Christ, will be revealed. He gave his life to free us from every kind of sin, to cleanse us, and to make us his very own people, totally committed to doing good deeds." Titus 2:11-14 New Living Translation.

We were not born-again just to go to church and live a life similar to those who are not saved. We were born again to be "like Christ" and have a life totally committed to doing good deeds. We were born anew to be His special people, totally freed from sin and prepared to do whatever He gives us to do. We should be a new breed of people, a people that stands out as being refreshingly different to others: a people that is not only redeemed, but sharing the light of Jesus with the rest of the world and bringing them into the fold. This is God's agenda for His people called after His Name.

God is a God of order: He equips His church to function in an orderly way. The Lord Jesus gave particular "gifts of ministry offices" to the church, in order to serve the congregation and to instruct others how to live and work for His glory. The people in the ministry offices were not intended to do all the work of the church. No, the ministry offices were given to teach the body how to do that work. There are five separate offices which have been appointed by our Lord Jesus Christ and these are listed in the passage below:

Now these are the gifts Christ gave to the church: the apostles, the prophets, the evangelists, and the pastors and teachers. Their responsibility is to equip God's people to do his work and build up the church, the body of Christ. This will continue until we all come to such unity in our faith and knowledge of God's Son that we will be mature in the Lord, measuring up to the full and complete standard of Christ. Ephesians 4:11-13 New Living Translation.

Ephesians 14- 16 continues: *"Then we will no longer be immature like children. We won't be tossed and blown about by every wind of new teaching. We will not be influenced when people try to trick us with lies so clever they sound like the truth. Instead, we will speak the truth in love, growing in every way more and more like Christ, who is the head of his body, the church. He makes the whole body fit together perfectly. As each part does its own special work, it helps the other parts grow, so that the whole body is healthy and growing and full of love."*

Christianity calls for the church to make preparation for multiplication. In other words, the church is to make disciples of men, women and boys and girls. This is the most effective way to rise up a fully-equipped army to overthrow the devil's plans. Many businesses use the tried and tested method of multiplication to grow and expand their business, called network marketing. I am sure that God would want His church to use a similar principle today, just as it successfully operated in the Book of Acts in the days of the early apostles.

1. An apostle was part of the church governance team. His responsibility was to raise up other churches and apostles, to train and teach them how to lead as the church grows.

2. A prophet was to bring the word of the Lord to the church and to teach the whole body to hear for themselves from God and live righteously.

3. An evangelist was to preach the gospel to gatherings and save the lost. He was to train the body how to share the good news of the Gospel to their friends and family.

4. A pastor was to shepherd the sheep and to provide a safe environment for young apostles, prophets, evangelists, pastors and teachers to practice their gifts and grow up to be all they were called to be.

5. A teacher was to teach the Word of God and encourage the congregation how to teach and learn for themselves.

If the five-fold ministry offices were working correctly, the church wouldn't have deception running rife within it, with divisions and fighting in its ranks. Instead, mature believers would nurture the baby Christians and everyone would be moving in unity and love. The church would be thriving in expansion. Every member of the church would be aware of their gifting and the calling that God had on their life.

As you might see, the church has a long way to go to be restored back to its original state. The body of Christ will be very powerful when it's focused onto eternal things and not on the things of the world, for these things pull us away from the things of God.

Paul said that: *"Since you have been raised to new life with Christ, set your sights on the realities of heaven, where Christ sits in the place of honor at God's right hand. Think about the things of heaven, not the things of earth. For you died to this life, and your real life is hidden with Christ in God." Colossians 3:1-3 New Living Translation.*

If you have understood what I have shared, you will realize that we, as a church, have to mature. I personally believe that the second coming of the Lord Jesus is fast approaching. Therefore, the whole church body needs to come into line and act and move as God intended. I believe that God will rise up many more teachers and practitioners of healing so that those of us who are currently suffering may be set free. Up till that day, I will endure the best I can; teach the best I can; and encourage the body as best as I can.

You may not realize it, but I have only devoted half the amount of space in writing about God's agenda than I wrote about Satan's agenda. However, you must realize that the majority of the Bible is about the story of God's dealing with man. Not nearly as much is recorded about the agenda Satan has for man.

Chapter 5
Have I Done Something Wrong to Deserve This?

Both Christians and non-Christians physically suffer in some way, and most people believe that their suffering results from wrong behavior. Religion teaches that sin causes sickness and many verses in the Bible seem to hint at that being the case. There are people who would teach you that you are suffering because of some sinful habit you presently have, or because of something that you have done in the past.

We need to always go back to our roots! God made man in perfection: He had no plan for us to ever experience suffering or death, in fact, the very opposite was true. Satan deceived man and sin and suffering entered the human race. Today, even though we might believe in Jesus and are part of His kingdom, the god of this world is still alive and active and he is using people and circumstances to do his bidding. There is good and evil operating in our world and we can very easily get wounded by the fiery darts of the devil.

When we suffer, we must realize that our mind can be our worst enemy, because Satan loves to play negative mind games. We might begin to think of all the people we know who are well, and they seem so much better off than us. Yet, in reality, we need to walk in the shoes of others to really know their personal pain and their actual circumstances.

Worse still, if you begin to compare our own "righteousness" to that of others who are not suffering, then the devil will quickly whisper to us that God is unfair. This type of reasoning may very well lead us to travel on a very dark road. It may take years for us to discover a new and better path. When we do, spiritual and physical restoration can take place in our life.

I was at a men's breakfast for leaders once and I prophesied over a pastor who was there. When I was finished, he told me he had a prophecy for me. I said "Great, please go ahead"

He said, "You have had a hard life marked with a lot of pain. In fact, you have had so much pain in your life that when you try and share it with other people, they don't seem to understand it. You have been very lonely and throughout life, you have had few friends. In fact, sometimes, Jesus was your only friend. Through all the suffering and loneliness, you have never, not even once, blamed God for your suffering. But all through your years, you have asked the question, "Why me, Lord?"

I was in tears as he said this. I nodded to say that I always wondered - why me?

He continued, "The Lord tells me that it was because of your suffering and loneliness that you drew so close to Him.

He wanted you very close to Him, so that you could be trusted with His words. He wanted you so close to Him so that when He spoke to you and told you to say something, that you would not change His words but speak faithfully for Him. There was no other way He could draw you so close to Him, so that you could be His mouthpiece."

I have to tell you - that day, my questions were answered! It was one of the most life-changing prophecies that I have ever received. I was amazed that the Lord said that I had never blamed Him for my suffering. I was surprised that the Lord needed me to have such a painful life so that I would be as close to Him that I am today.

In saying this, I want to emphatically clarify that the Lord never caused my suffering! My mental disorder manifested because of the trauma of my divorce and loss of custody for my young son. Severe mental and emotional breakdown triggered the mental health curse in my gene-line to manifest. Although the devil tried to close me down, I must admit that my own careless lifestyle choices helped him to do it.

Although I have never taken illicit drugs. The use of such mind-destroying drugs, together with abnormal sexual activity, is extremely prevalent in today's society. Both of these can very often be linked to mental health disorders. One can be the cause and the other the result of mental illness. Satan will use any form of "lack" or "over-indulgence" in our lives to pull us down and to make us feel unlovable.

I love the Lord and I honestly would not trade my relationship with Jesus for any other relationship. I enjoy a rich friendship with Jesus. He is very special to me and we have a close walk together. The Holy Spirit is very close to me. We walk everywhere together, whether I am doing the will of the Lord, or even if I am just doing my own thing. I know that God never leaves me.

Do you really believe that personal sin has caused your suffering and sickness? I guess you could rightly say this if you indulged in too many alcoholic drinks for your body to handle.

We must never ever lose sight of the truth that the wrath of God for the *collective sin of all mankind since Adam to the Second Coming* was once forever poured out onto the body of Jesus on the cross. Jesus was beaten, had his beard ripped out, was spat upon, was scourged, and hung on a tree for you and I. I believe that would certainly be enough punishment for any sin that you have committed, don't you agree?

We don't live in Old Testament days when God had to resort to using extreme punishment to pull His people back into line. The Holy Spirit didn't permanently indwell people back in those days so they didn't have inward spiritual understanding. Therefore, God had to use punishment in order to preserve them in much the same way a loving parent will discipline a toddler, otherwise they can easily put themselves in danger of being hurt.

The Bible clearly teaches that Jesus certainly suffered enough for all of us! When He presented His blood on the Mercy Seat in Heaven to the Father after the resurrection, God's anger against all sin was forever appeased and satisfied. Not only that, but every believer has been given the Holy Spirit and they, therefore, have spiritual understanding to be able to rightly discern the things of God, from the things of the world and the devil.

"Surely He has borne our griefs and carried our sorrows; yet we esteemed Him stricken, smitten by God, and afflicted. But He was wounded for our transgressions, He was bruised for our iniquities; the chastisement for our peace was upon Him, and by His stripes we are healed. All we like sheep have gone astray; we have turned, every one, to his own way; and the Lord has laid on Him the iniquity of us all." Isaiah 53:4-6.

The last line of this passage says that the Father laid the sin of all of us onto His Son Jesus.

This sin burden included every individual sin of all mankind! To put this in perspective: imagine if you were told that a huge inheritance was available to you and was placed in a bank safe, ready for your collection. All you needed was proof of identity and to turn up at the bank and claim your inheritance. However, you thought it was just some kind of scam or hoax, so you didn't bother contacting the bank. You would miss out on what you were legally entitled to, wouldn't you?

However, personal salvation and a future eternity in Heaven, is far better than any earthly inheritance placed in a bank somewhere. Yet, people either remain ignorant, or choose to not believe the full Gospel message. The average person lives their life as if Jesus had done nothing for them and in doing so, they fail to claim personal forgiveness of sin.

In fact, most people are so wrapped up in the things that they think are wonderful, that they are not even interested in the cross of Jesus! They just live their lives moment by moment and only acknowledge God as a hard taskmaster or as a fairy-tale character or when they are really upset about something. They will even go to a friend's funeral and reflect on the life of the deceased, but not give much thought on their own afterlife.

As believers, we can confidently know what happens after death and we don't fear God's wrath being put on us because of our sin. We know that the price of every sin that we have ever even thought about committing was laid on Jesus, as He hung on that dreadful cross.

Notice, too, that the passage above in Isaiah says that Jesus on the cross bore all our personal grief and sorrows! Therefore, we should place day to day burdens onto Him as well. We should give Jesus our sadness and let Him carry it for us, and receive His peace and His joy through His presence within us.

Jesus invited us to do this, He said: *"Come to Me, all you who labour and are heavy laden, and I will give you rest. Take My yoke upon you and learn from Me, for I am gentle and lowly in heart and you will find rest for your souls. For My yoke is easy and My burden is light." Matthew 11:28-30.*

At another time, Jesus said: *"Peace I leave with you, My peace I give to you; not as the world gives do I give to you. Let not your heart be troubled, neither let it be afraid." John 14:27.*

The world's peace is conditional and brief. God's peace is a perfect peace!

We know ourselves better than any other living person and it's so natural for us to blame ourselves for our sickness. We know what we have done wrong, and we are certainly aware of feeling our guilt. We think - surely this suffering and pain is the direct result of our own disobedience. We exclude ourselves from forgiveness by saying things like: "Sure, people can quote all that they want to, but I know in my heart how bad I have been. This sickness is my punishment, so I will just have to bear it."

No! God didn't mess up: He didn't have Jesus put to death for only part of our sins and the other part has to be dealt with by us! This kind of rationale is an error – it's a lie coming from the enemy. Satan's constant agenda is seeing us suffer. Sickness and suffering comes from his evil package of lies.

With that being said, despite what some people might say; God can actually use suffering to draw us closer to Him and refine our character. Mind you, He never causes suffering! Just like the example I used in my life that the pastor prophesied to me: *God has used my pain and suffering, or in other words, God has taken advantage of my pain and suffering* - to bring me closer to Him and keep me closer to Him, so that I can be His voice.

So nothing you have done wrong has caused God to bring sickness into your life.

Realize that some sicknesses and illnesses can be the natural consequences of our choice in lifestyle. It hasn't anything to do with God or the devil – we bring it upon ourselves! For example:

- A gay man who has unprotected sex may get aids.
- A person who continually gains excess weight may develop diabetes.
- A person who harbors bitterness and unforgiveness may develop cancers and other debilitating illnesses.
- An alcoholic can destroy his liver.
- Taking unprescribed drugs can cause mental illness.
- Lack of personal hygiene can cause infections and tooth decay, etc.

The point I am making is that sickness often comes from a careless lifestyle choice.

Yes, in the Old Covenant days, God did get very angry with disobedient people. We read in the Book of Psalms:

"God is a just judge, and God is angry with the wicked every day" Psalm 7:11.

The psalmist said: *"The boastful shall not stand in Your sight; You hate all workers of iniquity, You shall destroy those who speak falsehood; the Lord abhors the bloodthirsty and deceitful man." Psalm 5:5-6.*

I am so pleased that I don't live under the Old Covenant, aren't you? As believers, we have God's Holy Spirit living in us so we can boldly approach the Throne of God through a new and living way, not through the blood sacrifices of dead bulls and goats, but by the perfect and eternal sacrifice made once and for all on the cross of Calvary.

The night that He was betrayed, Jesus had gathered with His disciples for the last time, *"And He took bread, gave thanks and broke it, and gave it to them, saying, 'This is My body which is given for you; do this in remembrance of Me'. Likewise He also took the cup after supper, saying, 'This cup is the new covenant in My blood, which is shed for you.'" Luke 22:19-20.*

That night, Jesus instituted a New Covenant with us. Gone are the days of the Old Covenant.

Today, God is no longer an angry God! Today, God relates to us by His amazing grace! He certainly is deeply grieved at times, when man hurts man, but He has no more anger against those His son died for, and that's all of us, not just Christians!

In fact, God is no longer angry towards any of us, so why would He inflict us with sickness when Jesus suffered on the cross *for all our sin and sicknesses?* King David linked both these things in one verse - see Psalm 103:3. This is remarkable because David would have written this verse over seven hundred years before Christ came to die for us.

This has been a relatively new revelation to me, because most of my life, I really thought God was angry at me. When we lose sight of the fact that we live in post cross days and not pre-cross days, we open the door to the devil to play all sorts of horrible mind games with us. If you have allowed the devil to do this to you, begin asking God to give you a personal revelation about His grace or read my book on *Your Identity in Christ*.

Having said that, I believe that sickness, suffering and pain are all part of a fallen world.

We can be set free of these trials through faith and healing and I look forward to a day where many more of us will experience the freedom that Jesus died for. Until then, we should live a life where we are being a light to others and being salt to a dying world. If you personally know Jesus as your Savior and yet you suffer, give your hurts and pain to Him and let Him help you cope on a day to day basis. I know by experience that in doing so, you will be establishing a wonderful day to day relationship with Him.

Nevertheless, not a week goes by without my mental illness having an effect on me. I could just give up and feel sorry for myself and feel justified in doing that. But reacting that way does none of us any good. Instead, I choose to carve out times when I am feeling well to do things that God has given me to do and when it really gets all too much, I find myself just hibernating, tucked up in my bed.

I will challenge you like I challenge myself: What can you do for God and others despite your suffering? Spend some time thinking on that and then make up your mind to do it.

Chapter 6
Is This My Destiny?

Many people who feel trapped by suffering envisage their life's future and ask the painful questions, "Is this my life now? Is this all I have to look forward to?"

I remember losing my mind and being totally terrified with what I was seeing and thinking. I was locked up in the mental ward of a hospital and was not allowed out. Not only was I feeling weird in my head, but all the people I was locked up with, seemed that they too, were out of control. I struggled even with medication to get my life back to some sort of order, and in the midst of my confusion and mental anguish, I remember thinking: "Is this all there is to my life now?"

Not only did I have a mental illness, but I could no longer hold down a job. I was therefore placed on a disability pension, and although thankful for a steady income flow, I did feel the associated stigma of being on such a pension. When I met new people and they asked what I did for a living, I would tell them I didn't work, but was on a pension. The next question was "How come?" Being honest, I would tell them that I had a mental illness. Suddenly, I felt that they were looking at me differently and wanted to end the conversation.

Suffering too, can bring another stigma – fear! People don't want to catch your illness: they seem to be afraid that your problem will somehow come upon them, so they keep their distance. Others may feel uncomfortable simply because they are ignorant about mental health issues. They may want to pray for you, but don't really know how. People on the whole hate feeling out of their depth, yet they really do care for you.

Ignorance can be a curse. People don't want to accept that they may lack the faith-power to heal you, so often, they just draw away. Others may gather the courage to pray for you and when you are not healed, some of them can't handle it. Maybe they conclude that you lacked the faith to be healed and that your lack of faith may perhaps transfer onto them.

When you have been ill for a few years, you might seriously struggle with depression and worry about your future life. If you just focus on yourself and your circumstances, things can look very dim and if you are not careful, you will lose hope. You may even question the goodness of God. If you can identify with these things, I can testify out of experience that this is definitely the time to be focusing your thoughts onto Jesus and not onto yourself.

"Therefore, since we are surrounded by such a huge crowd of witnesses to the life of faith, let us strip off every weight that slows us down, especially the sin that so easily trips us up. And let us run with endurance the race God has set before us. We do this by keeping our eyes on Jesus, the champion who initiates and perfects

our faith. Because of the joy awaiting Him, He endured the cross, disregarding its shame. Now He is seated in the place of honor beside God's throne. Think of all the hostility He endured from sinful people; then you won't become weary and give up." Hebrews 12:1-3 (New Living Translation).

My Bible notes say: The heroes of faith are not spectators watching us from heaven; rather, their lives are "witnesses" to us, having successfully overcome. The Christian life is often likened to a race. Therefore, we are to lay aside anything that hinders our progress, particularly every form of sin.

Paul encourages all of us: *"Do you not know that those who run in a race all run, but one receives the prize? Run in such a way that you may obtain it." 1 Corinthians 9:24.*

Then, later in his life, as Paul remembers all the struggles he has endured, he confidently proclaims: *"I have fought the good fight. I have finished the race, I have kept the faith. Finally, there is laid up for me the crown of righteousness, which the Lord, the righteous Judge, will give to me on that Day, and not to me only but also to all who have loved His appearing." 2 Timothy 4:7-8.*

The Greek word for righteousness in this passage, means 'just' which is the quality of being right. The word suggests conformity to the revealed will of God in all respects. *"Dikaiosune"* means both judicial and gracious. God declares the believer righteous, in the sense of acquitting him, and imparts righteousness to him- see 1 Corinthians 5:21.

Many of us sing in church a very well-known chorus. Actually, this was the chorus that my mother sung to my dying grandmother moments before the Lord took her to glory.

"Turn your eyes upon Jesus,

Look full to His wonderful face,

And the things of earth, will grow strangely dim,

in the light of His glory and grace."

The original Hebrew word, "aphorao," used in Hebrews 12:2 for "looking," means undivided attention, looking away from all distractions in order to fix one's gaze on one object i.e. having eyes for no one but Jesus. When we lift our eyes from ourselves and focus our attention fully onto Jesus and the shame and suffering He endured for us, it never fails to uplift us because it will bring us into praise and thankfulness to His goodness to us. Then, we will truly discover that our problems actually dim in the light of His glory and grace.

Jesus set us such a high example. From a boy, He knew that He was going to suffer a horrific death and yet He continued through His youth, through His ministry years and went to the cross with joy in His heart, knowing what He was going to achieve *for all of us!* We need to think about Jesus, as Paul says and think of the hostility He faced so that we don't become weary and give up on life For a more detailed account of Jesus' life see my *book Kingdom Nuggets.*

Of course, the enemy will assail us with all kinds of negative thoughts: he has to be true to his evil nature. I know that even on my better days, the enemy is never too far away, trying to discourage me. The enemy wants us to dwell *on our life, and on our sadness and pain*. He wants us to feel that we are being treated unfairly by God and for us to turn away from God.

He wants us to think that sadness will disqualify us from having a productive life. Instead of fighting our born-again nature to press on and make do, and do good things with our life despite our setback, he wants us to give up in self-pity and just go on being sad.

If we focus on ourselves and our situation, life can become very glum. I have discovered that if I spend too much time thinking about my depression, my sleeping troubles, and my mania at other times, I would just give up on life. But instead of focussing on all the struggles in my life, I purposely set my mind on what the Holy Spirit wants me to do; on pleasing Jesus; and on other people. Make the choice to go on focusing on God and others despite your suffering and you too will discover the joy of doing the good works that God has for you to do.

"For we are His workmanship, created in Christ Jesus for good works, which God prepared beforehand that we should walk in them." Ephesians 2:10.

If God has already prepared good works for you and I to do, don't you think that we should set about doing them?

Your pain and suffering might be part of your life, but they should not define your life and your destiny! Your destiny is found in what you can do for God and others despite your suffering. I, like many before me, have discovered that my life is a whole lot better when my focus is on God and others and not on myself.

God might want you to encourage others through sharing your story on a blog or in a book. People can find great hope and strength when someone who suffers in life shares positive things with them. As a believer, I find that the best people to speak to when I am suffering are other believers who have suffered like me, yet they have gone on and done great things for God. These are truly inspirational people!

I finished writing a book the other day called "Living for Eternity" and I attended a prophetic class on Skype. A person prophesied to me that I was to begin my next book right away.

Before the two hour class was over, I had been given the title of this book on pain and suffering by the Holy Spirit and all the chapter titles. I had not ever thought of writing such a book. Yet, the Lord knew that my life of suffering had prepared me to write on the subject and bring some much needed encouragement to others.

I partly feel unqualified to write on all the chapter titles, but I feel that God is perhaps testing me. However, because the Holy Spirit has led me, I'm confident that He will give me many of the words to say. Therefore, I will continue doing my assignment, knowing that I will learn more about the subject in the process.

Sometimes, we tend to forget that God has already planned the works for us to do since before the foundation of the earth. We need to confidently allow the Holy Spirit to lead us and empower us to achieve great things, that otherwise would be impossible for us to do. I say this because I feel that few believers really trust the Holy Spirit's lifetime commitment to us and to the Father, to guide us in the things of God both before and after salvation.

Paul testified *that in his own weaknesses, he was strong!* Obviously, he knew by personal experience that it was only through the help and power of the Holy Spirit that he triumphed though his weaknesses. What was true for Paul is true for us today as well, because our Lord Jesus Christ is the same yesterday, today and forever according to Hebrews 13:8.

Paul tells us that *"God has chosen the foolish things of the world to put to shame the wise, and God has chosen the weak things of the world to put to shame the things which are mighty."* 1 Corinthians 1:27.

Later, we read: *"For the wisdom of this world is foolishness with God. For it is written, He catches the wise in their own craftiness"* 1 Corinthians 3:19 (A quote from Job 5:13).

"Craftiness" means versatile cleverness, sophisticated cunning, arrogance, shrewdness.

- The devil used craftiness when he questioned Eve about God's Word. (Genesis 3:4)

- The Pharisees displayed craftiness when they tried to trick Jesus with their questions.

- False teachers display craftiness by their ability to twist Scripture to a false meaning.

- The devil uses craftiness by the self-entrapment of the "worldly" wise.

God gives us faith for a very good reason. We are called, no matter who we are, to do good works for Him through helping others. James had these thought-provoking words to say:

"What does it profit, my brethren, if someone says he has faith but does not have works? Can faith save him? If a brother or sister is naked and destitute of daily food, and one of you says to them, "Depart in peace, be warmed and filled," but you do not give them the things which are needed for the body, what does it profit? Thus also faith by itself, if it does not have works, is dead. James 2: 14-17.

Many unbelievers have had horrific things happen to them, but they refuse to engage in self-pity and they just push on in life. These people may not necessarily give glory to God, but their drive to succeed is so uplifting.

Then there are mighty and victorious Christians, who do give glory to God even in their sufferings. I have in mind a DVD about a young man who had a tragic birth defect. On the cover of his testimony DVD is written:

"Life Without Limbs" by Nick Vujicic.

"From no limbs, to no limits."

"Life's greater purpose."

On the back cover of his DVD, Nick has quoted a well-known Bible verse from the Old Testament: *"For I know the plans I have for you" declares the Lord, "plans to prosper you and not to harm you, plans to give you hope and a future." Jeremiah 29:11.*

I have at times quoted this verse to myself many times, but it took on far more meaning after I watched this amazing Christian "brother" overcoming his terrible disabilities. His attitude is truly inspirational! He is happily married and is a father. I highly recommend that you look up his website address LIFEWITHOUTLIMBS.ORG.

Regardless of what any of my readers may suffer, I guarantee that seeing and hearing Nick's incredible testimony will lift your spirit to a new high! Therefore, try not to glibly verbalize: "Is this my destiny?" Instead, like Nick Vujicic, think about what you can do for God and others, despite your hard life. Like me, you may be pleasantly surprised at what God will enable you to do.

Chapter 7
Am I a New Testament Job?

The author and the date of the Book of Job have not been firmly established. Some believe Job himself wrote it while others suggest, perhaps Moses, Solomon, or one of the prophets may have been the author. However, the overall joint-theme of Job is the suffering of the Godly; and the sovereignty of God. The key words in the book are 'sin' and 'righteousness.'

Its opening words tell us that: *"There was a man in the land of Uz, whose name was Job; and that man was blameless and upright, and one who feared God and shunned evil."*

Some people suffer horrendous things and may even consider that they are somewhat like Job. I can understand their thinking, because Satan hasn't changed - he still comes to cause havoc upon us today. However, I definitely wouldn't call my own life one that was blameless and one that shunned evil because I have done many bad things.

Chapter one continues: *"And seven sons and three daughters were born to him. Also, his possessions were seven thousand sheep, three thousand camels, five hundred yoke of oxen, five hundred female donkeys, and a very large household, so that this man was the greatest of all the people of the East. And his sons would go and feast in their houses, each on his appointed day, and would send and invite their three sisters to eat and drink with them. So it was, when the days of feasting had run their course, that Job would send and sanctify them, and he would rise early in the morning and offer burnt offerings according to the number of them all. For Job said, "It may be that my sons have sinned and cursed God in their hearts." Thus Job did regularly." Job 1:2-7.*

Then, verse 8 reinforces the reality of the opening verse: *"Then the Lord said to Satan, "Have you considered My servant Job, that there is none like him on the earth, a blameless and upright man, one who fears God and shuns evil?"*

It's important to note that God calls Job blameless, and that there was none like him in all the earth. God says that Job shunned evil, which means he resisted sinning. It's important to know that Job made sacrifices for his sons in case they, unlike him, had sinned. Job must have been extremely confident in his own heart and mind that he had not sinned. This to me makes Job extremely unique.

In fact, the whole reason Satan sought God's permission to smite Job's family and to hurt him, was that Job was blameless! Satan thought Job would sin if given enough rope. We discover however that Job didn't sin even through all the devastating tragedies that beset him.

My testimony,

I have intimated earlier that perhaps Satan has been permitted by God to unleash his torments, as a way to draw me closer to God. At times, I even fear that my life may continue to be a struggle with that end in mind. However, even in writing this, a verse readily comes to my mind: "Let no one say when he is tempted, 'I am tempted by God' for God cannot be tempted by evil, nor does He Himself tempt anyone." James 1:13.

Therefore, we are not to be deceived: "But each one is tempted when he is drawn away by his own desires and enticed. Then, when desire has conceived, it gives birth to sin; and sin, when it is full grown, brings forth death." James 14-15.

Just writing these things have given me clarity - my professed fear of always struggling is not of God. Why? Because I know that God is a good God all the time! Therefore, my fear of future struggle must come from the demonic world, because God is gracious to me always! God's kind of fear is a reverent and holy fear, as clearly implied in the following passage.

"Therefore, since we are receiving a kingdom which cannot be shaken, let us have grace, by which we may serve God acceptably with **reverence and Godly fear**. For our God is a consuming fire." Hebrews 12:28-29 (Emphasis mine).

The Apostle Paul wrote to young Timothy: "For the grace of God that brings salvation has appeared to all men, teaching us that, denying ungodliness and worldly lusts, we should live soberly, righteously, and godly in the present age, looking for the blessed hope and glorious appearing of our Great God and Savior Jesus Christ, who gave Himself for us, that He might redeem us from every lawless deed and purify for Himself His own special people, zealous for good works." Titus 2:11-14.

*I'm so pleased that God wanted me to write this book, because He has made me constantly aware of His awesome grace in my life. As I think about God's grace in my life, I recall that John Bevere, author of "Extraordinary Grace" says that faith in God is like a pipeline that carries God's precious grace-power to us, which will then enables us to live a God-pleasing life. The words in Ephesians 2:8 come to mind, "For by grace you have been saved **through** faith, and that not of yourselves; it is the gift of God."(Emphasis mine).*

I also know that when God from Heaven looks down at any Christian, He sees them only as being "in Christ" so He loves them like He own beloved Son.

The Book of Job tells us about a real person who lived on earth! We know this because the Prophet Ezekiel refers to Job together with two other Old Testament saints, namely Noah and Daniel. We can see this in Ezekiel 14:14 and again in verse 20.

The story of Job is about a wealthy Gentile who continually acknowledged God by the name of *Shaddai – the Almighty* even in the very sad times of his life. Job knew the secret resting place of the Lord, even despite Satan's effort to turn him away from God. Therefore, Job knew the all-sufficiency of His God – he knew that His God was eternally capable of being all that he would ever need. Job knew that in the hidden place of God's rest, his soul would not be moved regardless of what was stolen from him and placed upon him. The Lord lovingly referred to Job as *"My servant Job"* in verse eight of the first Chapter.

This book is not just a sad story. No, it's far more than that! My Bible notes say that; "Job's story is set against the backdrop of the potential sufferings, struggles, and sorrows of real life and the triumph and vindication of faithful integrity, even when dealing with difficult questions and tragic situations."

We are to know that the entire Word of God was written for our benefit, so we can be confident that within all its pages, we will find relevant messages for us today. Job suffered pain in his own body; he suffered financial loss of material possessions and the agonizing loss of close family; he suffered misunderstanding by his associates; he suffered condemnation and was unduly criticised by others. Although his faith in the goodness of God was severely tested, yet he held onto this belief because in his heart, he knew it to be true.

Satan believed if he threw enough of his poisonous darts into Job, that this "blameless" man would curse God and he would no longer be special in God's sight. However, Job gave an excellent summary of defence. Job states that his suffering was not due to his sin, but had some deeper reason, which only God knew.

Job knew his former prosperity was the direct result of his lifestyle of piety and benevolence and had therefore reasoned that his prosperity would continue until he died. Job closes his discourse by again saying that he is guilty of no hypocrisy, either outwardly or secretly in his heart. His final and firmest vow of innocence is recorded in Job 31:24-40.

I pray that we could all strive to become such a devoted believer in God's goodness as Job was. We should all strive like Job to become a great worker for love and social justice. This is what the Lord our God requires from us all. Micah 6:8 tells us to do justly; to love mercy and to walk humbly with our God.

The New King James Spirit Filled Life Bible has a "Truth-in-action" section at the end of each book. I will briefly state just some of the lessons we can adopt from the Book of Job.

Chapter 1:6-12. God always knows exactly what we can handle and He will never push us beyond our capability. God permits testing for the purpose of strengthening faith and character.

Chapter 1:22. Know that God is with us, even in the midst of intense trials. He has promised to never leave us in Hebrews 12:5b.

Chapter 2:7. We are to recognize that a demonic power may be involved in our suffering or affliction; but we are also to remember, *"He who is in you is greater than he who is in the world." 1 John 4:4.*

Chapter 9:32-3. We are to rejoice in the knowledge that Jesus Christ is our Mediator and Advocate with the Father. 1Timothy 2:5 and 1 John 2:1.

<u>Chapter 13:15.</u> As Christians, we can confidently trust in "Who" God is based on what "His Word" has revealed Him to be. Jesus Christ is the "Living" Word of God and the Holy Spirit personally reveals Jesus to us.

<u>Chapter 16:1-4</u>. We are never to assume that someone's trial is a result of sin or judgment. All of us need *encouragement* to overcome trials, not any form of condemnation! Be aware that the Holy Spirit convicts of sin by giving us a little "check" in our spirit. Demons, however, put condemnation onto people so that they feel unworthy of God's love.

<u>Chapter 19:25.</u> Hold fast to Jesus, our Redeemer. Be comforted knowing that He is well able to *redeem any circumstance!* Whether in hardship, suffering, being wrongly treated or bitterly disappointed, or in any other negative situation, Christians can be assured that God can make all things work out for good for them. We need to personally claim Romans 8:28.

<u>Chapter 31:1.</u> Make a personal commitment to keep your eyes pure. Look upon only those things that are honorable to the Lord and are consistent with holiness. The Psalmist personally pleads to God *"Turn away my eyes from looking at worthless things and revive me in Your ways." Psalm 119:37.*

<u>Chapter 40:4-5.</u> Humble yourself before the Lord just as Job did. He encountered God's majesty and holiness and it left him deeply aware of his sin and his inability to justify himself. – See Isaiah 6:5-7. The devil wants to oppress us,

like Job, we are to *"submit to God, resist the devil and he will flee from us." James 4:7.*

<u>Chapter 42:5.</u> Simply hearing about God is not enough! We need to have a personal encounter with the Living God. This will enable us to develop intimacy with Him and to perceive and really know Him for ourselves.

<u>Chapter 42:7-8.</u> We are to pursue diligently the understanding of God's perspective when trying to apply truth to a given situation. Though Job's friends spoke truths, they incorrectly applied them and falsely accused their sad friend. They did not speak rightly about God, nor did they understand God's perspective. As a result, they provoked God's wrath! Understand that an honest struggle on faith's journey is more honoring to God than religious sounding talk or mere religious observance.

<u>Chapter 42:10.</u> We are to pray for those who misunderstand us. Note: God redeemed all that Satan had earlier taken *when Job prayed for those who had falsely accused him*. Forgiveness, therefore, is a key to restoration. Matthew 5:44 and Romans 12:14.

Job was not only blameless in the sight of God, but he was like the "king of his region" and princes and other kings answered to him. Our world would be a great place if every city had a person like Job ruling it.

Satan would like us to think that God has allowed the devil to destroy our joy in life because of our sin. But this is not so. Sure, we may have been hurt, we may suffer, but it's never because we have sinned because Christ took all the punishment for man's sin! This fact has already been settled in Heaven by God Himself!

Job was a righteous man of God, but he lived long before the New Covenant which was eternally secured by the blood of Jesus Christ. Yes, God wants us to strive to become blameless in our soul area, but in our born-again spirit, we are *already* blameless. God sees us as spiritual people! The devil can NEVER interfere with our perfect born-again spirit, which in God's sight, is our true identity.

Chapter 8
Finding Joy in the Journey

To me, living a life without purpose would be a very sad life. I feel that I have been very fortunate to have found my calling in teaching and writing books. Even though I suffer, I find great joy in expressing my faith in God and seeing people buy my books because I always want to share my belief in the absolute goodness of God.

It really encourages me when people write to me and tell me one of my books impacted them. I am always blessed when I see a new positive review on Amazon for one of my books. God is the author of our life and He wants to show us the path that our life is to take.

"You will show me the path of life; In Your presence is fullness of joy; At Your right hand are pleasures forevermore." Psalm 16:11.

This verse declares that God will show us the path that we are to walk on. Proverbs 3:5 assures us that when we trust and honor God and not lean on our own understanding, that He will direct our paths. This above verse in Psalm 16 reveals to us that in the presence of God is the fullness of joy!

I have to agree, walking in the presence of God does bring my life much joy and peace. God is absolutely amazing and the feelings that He can give us are so positive and uplifting. Having the ability to praise God and enter into His presence is something He has placed inside of us. That's why so many unbelievers search for some god in their life. Our human spirit is longing to be fulfilled. God created us to have relationship and fellowship with Him.

When I suffer depression, it's harder to feel the presence of God, yet when depression goes, I am so happy to walk in His presence. God is such a good God. I remember way back in the 1980's, there was a simple Christian chorus that as a young teenager, I just loved to sing:

> "God is so good. He took my sin. Now I am free. He's so good to me."

Sometimes, when you are suffering, and you reflect on your life, it is good to determine in your heart to reflect on God's goodness in your life. What are some of these things that He had done for you? Just reflecting on them will lift your spirit.

I have discovered that praising God is like medicine for my soul. I realize that some people might even think: "There's nothing good in my life!" That would be a sad, sad state to be in, because if you asked people who really knew you, they would tell you many wonderful things about your life. Satan has just hidden them from your memory because of your present state of mind.

King Solomon had discovered a wonderful reality: *"A merry heart does good, like medicine, but a broken spirit dries the bones." Proverbs 17:22.*

Ask God to remind you of the blessings you already have. Besides God, I can readily think of three good things and they all start with the letter "F" for fun, friendship and fellowship.

> Family - can be a good thing in your life.
>
> Friends - can be a good thing in your life.
>
> Facebook - can even be a good thing in your life.

Though if your family are mean to you, or you have no friends and you don't enjoy Facebook, your life in my opinion could be pretty grim. If I was in that state, I would try and find a place where people were worse off than I, and then I would go and minister some love to them. In that way, I would be lifting up my spirit and their spirit in a positive way.

I think it's true to say, "There is always someone worse off than us" It's not just a cliché! When you just focus on yourself, you can become very sad and despondent. Though if you pick yourself up for a moment and think of how you can make a positive difference in the life of someone else who may be worse off than you, you might have found a good way to escape your own doom and gloom.

Many people spend hours weeping all alone. Life can be so painful, especially if you feel no one cares. But God truly does care and so would others if we just reached out a little. At my church, we sing a couple of songs from time to time with this promise in it. *"Weeping may endure for a night but joy comes in the morning."* These words come from Psalm 30:5.

Believe me: I know that it's important to praise God even in the midst of a hard time. Praise is a very effective spiritual tool for any believer to use against the devil and his attacks on us. Worship to God can often set us free from sadness, because worship brings the presence of God. His peace and His joy can overwhelm us and we can be swept up into God's loving embrace. There is simply no better place to be!

I realize that I am very fortunate that I can see visions and have Jesus meet me and speak to me in my sad times and in my good times. Meeting with Jesus can be so encouraging and knowing His love for me is so comforting. He is so good to me! I can accept that not all people are fortunate enough to see visions, but I know that many of you can feel Jesus' presence if you make up your mind to worship God, even in the hard times that you face.

It's so very important to transfer your prime focus from yourself and onto God.

Make a commitment to yourself that you will worship God. Satan will try to stop you, but press on anyway. I know from experience that my mind and emotions will not want me to worship, but I do it anyway. Because I know that once

I make that decision and put it into action, then the Holy Spirit will cause me to enter into heartfelt worship. Believe me, I have been there many times. I strongly advise you to praise God in your sad times, as I am confident that like me, you too will experience a truly great release. You could repeat the following passage out loud to God as a prayer:

"Send out Your light and Your truth; let them guide me. Let them lead me to Your holy mountain, to the place where You live. There I will go to the altar of God, to God—the source of all my joy. I will praise you with my harp, O God, my God! Why am I discouraged? Why is my heart so sad? I will put my hope in God! I will praise him again my Savior and my God! Psalm 43:3-5. New Living Translation.

Here, David admits that his heart was discouraged and sad and what did he do? He went before God and praised Him and set his heart free of sorrow. When we read this, it makes a lot of sense to worship God when things are tough. God really loved David, he is known as a man after God's Own heart. We have to purposely do the same, as no one can do it for us.

Often, when I am on the internet, I play worship music and my spirit gets lifted to another place. You don't need to know all the words of the song to be encouraged by worship music, but if you want to know the words, you can look them up by searching for the lyrics and then it's great to just sing along to them.

You don't have to wait till Sunday or the day you attend church to enter into worship. You don't have to only enter the presence of God once a week. You can be in His presence each day. I honestly don't know what I would do if I didn't have the presence of God in my life.

However, I do know one thing: even if I could not feel the presence of Jesus, I would speak to Him often and be encouraged by the words He speaks back to me, and I would spend a lot of time in His Word.

I have a friend who cannot feel the presence of God. She suffers with depression and though she used to feel the presence of God, she doesn't feel it anymore. It would be really hard to cope and to go on if that was me. Mind you, I do suffer sometimes from depression and I tend to just sleep my way through it. But on other days when I feel a little down, I often immerse myself in helping others. I know that I will receive comfort from the smiles of others and their vocal appreciation. Serving others allows me to be able to wait on God to lift my soul area, so that I can feel his presence again.

David speaks a lot about joy. Psalm 98:4 tells us to: *"Shout joyfully to the Lord, all the earth; Break forth in song, rejoice, and sing praises."* It definitely makes sense to praise God when you really think about it.

You might be so sad and depressed that the last thing you want to do is to praise God and thank Him for your life. But believe me, it's best to work through and past that feeling, and do it anyway! Our born-again spirit is at home when we are in communion with the Spirit of God. Our whole life can be changed by spending time in the Word of God and singing to Him. Not only will singing worship songs and choruses bring life to your spirit, but the words of Scripture in the songs actually changes us. Our soul will begin to rejoice as well.

Years ago, I had a sleep disorder where I slept up to eighteen hours each day and even if I did get out of bed earlier, I would be back in bed within a few minutes. This amount of sleep left me chronically depressed when I did get up. Each day was the same, day after day, year after year. It was mental and spiritual agony. My emotions became so sad.

However, after a few months, I found a way I could fight it. I could stay up all night and write articles on all sorts of subjects. It would take me about an hour to write a four page article so I would write about four articles each night and watch DVD's. I would stay up for a few days without sleep and enter into an extremely high state called mania. Then, I would have a little bit of happiness. Thinking back, some of those articles I posted on the web at that stage in my life would have had elements of "mania" in them, I'm sure.

This sleep disorder would not leave me despite much prayer. It was so devastating and painful that when I worshipped at church each week, I would just weep. In the process of writing articles and even in my weeping, I realize now that I was actually sowing good seed for others according to the Word of God.

"Those who sow in tears shall reap in joy. He who continually goes forth weeping, bearing seed for sowing, shall doubtless come again with rejoicing, bringing his sheaves with him. Psalm 126:5-6.

God uses my articles still today and people are still being blessed. The Holy Spirit taught me how to play worship music and sit down for hours to write, and now today, I find that writing books is a whole lot easier, because God had earlier conditioned my mind. Today, hopefully, many people are being blessed not only by the small postings I write, but by my books as well. Nearly every week during worship times at church, tears run down my face, as I am still sowing in tears, but there is much joy in my life today.

My Bible notes say that tears and brokenness can be victorious warfare, because tears in Scripture play a unique role in spiritual breakthrough. In Scripture, we discover that the planting of seeds, accompanied by a spirit of brokenness, will not only bring a spiritual harvest of results, but will leave the sower with a spirit of rejoicing in the process.

The above Scripture in Psalm 126, along with numerous others, might be termed a ministry of tears which have been called "Liquid Prayer." Passion in spiritual warfare is clearly needed.

I cry easily. God once told me in a prophecy that the effect that I have on earth will never be measured by man or by me. He said it is only when I get to Heaven that I will see the effect that I had on earth. This prophecy gave me so much peace and joy.

We all need to discover the particular thing in life that gives us purpose and brings joy to us. We need to look outside of ourselves and find a way how our life can bless God and others. It is only in this way that some of us will find freedom from sadness and suffering. There are people waiting for encouragement from us. No one is free of hurt and even those who seem to have it all together could very well be encouraged by you and your story.

Paul says that the Christian life should be full of righteousness, peace and joy. *"For the kingdom of God is not eating and drinking, but righteousness and peace and joy in the Holy Spirit. For he who serves Christ in these things is acceptable to God and approved by men."* Romans 14:17.

God does not want our life is to be an ongoing pity party. Instead, we can deliberately choose to shake off the gloom from ourselves and rise up and make a positive difference in our area of influence. We just need to make an effort and God will give us the strength. There is no point in wallowing in personal sadness. For me personally, in sad times: it's time for me to visit a soup kitchen and spread some cheer. Discover ways that suit your personality, to rise up and minister to others in the way that God has individually wired you.

I awoke at 1:00 this morning, because I slept too much yesterday. After going to the bathroom, I couldn't go back to sleep. I decided that God must have wanted me up, so I went down to the all-night gas station for milk. After drinking coffee, I settled down to write.

The Holy Spirit spoke to me and told me what verses to use in the first chapter of my new book I had started. I could have stayed in bed, tossed and turned and got upset that I could not sleep, but that would have only added to my frustration. Besides, I wouldn't have written four chapters of my book.

Every single day, we have choices to make. We may be in a difficult position and choose not do anything about it and just stay sad. Or we can choose to do something for others, feel better and have a sense of achievement with our lives.

Paul was praying for present and future believers and when I read one of his epistles, I always think that God is just talking to me personally. These are his words that God wants for me and my reader to adhere to: *"That you may walk worthy of the Lord, fully pleasing Him, being fruitful in every good work and increasing in the knowledge of God; strengthened with all might, according to His glorious power, for all patience and long-suffering with joy; giving thanks to the Father who has qualified us to be partakers of the inheritance of the saints in the light." Colossians 1:10-12.*

Are you fruitful in every good work? Are you walking worthy of the Lord being fully pleasing to Him? Have you been strengthened with the Holy Spirit according to His power in you? Have you been released with patience, long-suffering and joy?

We need to take steps to live a life that is not only pleasing to us but pleasing to God. There can be much joy in the journey. If it were not so, the Holy Spirit would not have had me write this chapter and I would not be able to testify of my own joy in the process.

Chapter 9
Some Impossible Cases in the Bible

You may have suffered for so long and your illness might be so bad that for you, future healing seems to be totally impossible. For this reason, I thought we would visit some stories in the Bible where Jesus broke new ground. Jesus not only had the ability to forgive sin, but He did other amazing miracles as well. Let's look at some of them in Mark's Gospel.

- The 1st miracle demonstrates that Jesus has authority over nature itself. This miracle can be found in Mark 4:35-41

Jesus had been sitting in a fishing boat and He began to teach a large crowd of people on the shore. He shared with them in detail the Parable of the Sower and gave an explanation of what the parable was all about and then He taught other parables to the waiting crowd.

[35] *One the same day, when evening had come, He said to them* (His disciples) *"Let us cross over to the other side."* [36] *Now when they had left the multitude, they took Him along in the boat as He was. And other little boats were also with Him.* [37] *And a great windstorm arose, and the waves beat into the boat, so that it was already filling.*

[38] *But He was in the stern, asleep on a pillow. And they awoke Him and said to Him, 'Teacher, do You not care that we are perishing?'* [39] *Then He arose and rebuked the wind, and said to the sea, "peace, be still!" And the wind ceased and there was a great calm.* [40] *But He said to them, "Why are you so fearful? How is it that you have no faith?"* [41] *And they feared exceedingly, and said to one another, "Who can this be, that even the wind and the sea obey Him!"*

Earlier, Jesus had pointed out in His Parable of the Sower that every Word of God is a "seed" that we are to plant in our heart, so that it will bear fruit in its own time. Jesus spoke about four different kinds of ground that the seed might be planted in. The ground represents four different reactions of a human heart when God's Word is presented to any hearer.

Jesus stressed the importance of hearing and understanding all the many "seed-truths" found in God's Word. God wants us to be aware that all of us have unknowingly planted negative seeds from the mouths of others or even by our own mouth, into the garden of our heart. But God wants us to plant the incorruptible seed of His truth in our heart, so that positive outcomes will be produced in our life. Every Word of God is a good seed that will produce good fruit, when we plant it deep into our heart.

Being tired from His day's teaching, Jesus was happy to rest in the bottom of the boat after He had instructed the disciples to cross over to the other side of the Sea of Galilee.

However, a savage storm developed which terrified His disciples as more water was surging into their boat than they could possibly bail out. They feared that they would all drown! Yet, they saw their sleeping Master peacefully, curled up as if nothing was untoward.

In absolute panic and even in anger that Jesus had not been helping them bail out the water, the terrified disciples woke Him up and straight away accused him of being neglectful by saying: "Don't you care that we perish?" Jesus stood up and with much authority in His voice, He first rebuked the wind and then spoke directly to the threatening waves, by proclaiming just three small words: "Peace, be still!" The wind and the waves immediately dropped and there was a great calm. (Mark 4:39)

As verse 41 says, *"And they feared exceedingly, and said to one another, "Who can this be, that even the wind and the sea obey Him!"*

Jesus had addressed the "unbelief" in His disciples by saying: "Why are you so fearful? How is it that you have no faith? He was astonished that the day's teaching had fallen on deaf ears.

When He had said to them, *"Let us cross over to the other side"* in Mark 4:35, He had deliberately planted a "seed" that they could rely on. Jesus wanted that seed to be planted deep in their hearts, so that they would not stress when the upcoming storm threatened them.

Even though He had earlier gone to such great lengths to explain how important it was to hear and take into our heart, the Word of God, they had obviously forgotten what He had said. He had not said: "Let's go half way over and drown!" No, He had purposely given a positive affirmation: *"Let us cross over to the other side."* Yet His pupils had totally dismissed His Word and let their emotions cripple them with fear. Jesus was amazed at their lack of faith and probably felt He had wasted His whole day's teaching on His pupils.

Jesus had wanted his disciples to exercise the authority they had in knowing Him. They could have spoken to the wind and the waves and commanded them to calm down *in His Name!* He had been training these twelve men so that when He was no longer around, they could continue teaching by example, how the Kingdom of God works. He was relying on them to eventually start an ongoing, thriving church on earth. He had spent much time investing in their lives. Maybe, He was tempted to think: "Have I made a mistake in choosing these guys?

They most likely, very soberly and quietly, continued on their journey across the lake, with each man silently going over in their mind the day's activities. Finally, they reached their destination where Jesus knew that His Father had a major work for Him to do.

- The 2nd miracle demonstrated that Jesus has authority over the demonic world. (See Mark 5:1-20 below.) This story continues immediately after the storm episode.

[1] *Then they came to the other side of the sea, to the country of the Gadarenes.* [2] *And when He had come out of the boat, immediately there met Him out of the tombs a man with an unclean spirit,* [3] *who had his dwelling among the tombs; and no one could bind him, not even with chains,* [4] *because he had often been bound with shackles and chains. And the chains had been pulled apart by him, and the shackles broken in pieces; neither could anyone tame him.* [5] *And always, night and day, he was in the mountains and in the tombs, crying out and cutting himself with stones.*

[6] *When he saw Jesus from afar, he ran and worshiped Him.* [7] *And he cried out with a loud voice and said, "What have I to do with You, Jesus, Son of the Most High God? I implore You by God that You do not torment me."*

[8] *For He said to him, "Come out of the man, unclean spirit!"* [9] *Then He asked him, "What is your name?" And he answered, saying, "My name is Legion; for we are many."* [10] *Also he begged Him earnestly that He would not send them out of the country.*

[11] *Now a large herd of swine was feeding there, near the mountains.* [12] *So all the demons begged Him, saying, "Send us to the swine, that we may enter them."* [13] *And at once Jesus gave them permission. Then the unclean spirits went out and entered the swine (there were about two thousand); and the herd ran violently down the steep place into the sea, and drowned in the sea.*

[14] *So those who fed the swine fled, and they told it in the city and in the country. And they went out to see what it was that had*

happened. *[15] Then they came to Jesus, and saw the one who had been demon-possessed and had the legion, sitting and clothed and in his right mind. And they were afraid. [16] And those who saw it told them how it happened to him who had been demon-possessed, and about the swine. [17] Then they began to plead with Him to depart from their region.*

[18] And when He got into the boat, he who had been demon-possessed begged Him that he might be with Him. [19] However, Jesus did not permit him, but said to him, "Go home to your friends, and tell them what great things the Lord has done for you, and how He has had compassion on you." [20] And he departed and began to proclaim in Decapolis all that Jesus had done for him; and all marvelled." Mark 5: 1-20.

Now let's look at this incident. In Mark 5:7-9, we read: *[7] "And he cried out with a loud voice and said, 'What have I to do with You, Jesus, Son of the Most High God? I implore you by God that You do not torment me.' [8] For He said to him, 'Come out of the man, unclean spirit!' [9] Then He asked him, 'What is your name?' And he answered, 'My name is Legion; for we are many.'"*

This was not the actual man's voice speaking to Jesus. No! This loud voice came from a terrified demon living inside of the man, for the demon had instantly recognised "Who" Jesus was and the authority that He carried.

That is very interesting isn't it? This story proves that demons can recognise the Spirit of God in a Christian - and they know that the Spirit of God has far more authority than they have! Yet, many Christians are not aware of the authority that they actually possess "in Christ." However, we are to know that on the cross, Jesus won this authority for all future believers. On the cross, Jesus had made a public spectacle of Satan according to Colossians 2:15 - *"Having disarmed principalities and powers, He made a public spectacle of them, triumphing over them in it."*

A demon is a fallen angel. When Satan wanted God's position in Heaven, he led a large number of angels to rebel against God's authority to rule. As a result, God cast these warring angels out of Heaven, so they came to earth. Just like a massive organized military army, these disgruntled demons have various ranks of authority, under Satan himself. This invisible spiritual force wars continually with those whom Jesus died for. (See Ephesians 6: 10-12)

Therefore, though the world is becoming increasingly selfish and violent, we are to realize that it is not man who is our *real enemy*, but rather the unseen spiritual beings deceiving and controlling people to hurt and destroy each other, so as to grieve the very heart of God.

When Jesus asked this demon his name, the demon answered "Legion." Demons do not want to be disembodied! Because demons don't have a physical body of their own, they operate like unseen "spiritual squatters" in any available earthly body. If they cannot find an available human who opens the door to them, the bodies of other creatures can suffice.

In verse 9, this demon told Jesus *"My name is Legion; for we are many."* What did he mean by this? Put into context, we are to know that at full strength, a Roman "legion" numbered 6,000 soldiers. The name "Legion" had come to signify a well-organized group possessing great power. Therefore, there could have been thousands of demons "squatting" in this particular human body. No wonder no one wanted to be anywhere near this violent and crazy man!

However, for us today, it is wonderful to know that demonic spiritual beings are actually terrified of Spirit-filled Christians. Demons automatically know that the power in a believer is far greater than their power. *"You are of God, little children, and have overcome them, because He who is in you* (The Holy Spirit) *is greater than he* (Satan) *who is in the world."* 1John 4:4.

Believers by faith have chosen to believe and submit themselves to God. Demons too believe, but rather than submit to God, they just tremble in fear. (See James 2:19) Legion appeals to Jesus to let them go into the herd of swine (pigs) nearby and Jesus agreed to their request.

"Now a large herd of swine was feeding there, near the mountains. So all the demons begged Him, saying, "Send us to the swine, that we may enter them." And at once Jesus gave them permission. Then the unclean spirits went out and entered the swine (there were about two thousand); and the herd ran violently down the steep place into the sea, and drowned in the sea." Mark 5:11-13.

My Bible notes suggest that perhaps Jesus allowed the demons to enter the pigs because He was teaching an object lesson to the people of the region, who were obviously more concerned with the loss of property than rejoicing over the deliverance of one of their countrymen. Clearly Jesus values people far more than property.

This now free man was so thankful to Jesus that all he wanted was to become one of Jesus' disciples and to follow the Rabbi everywhere He went. However, Jesus knew that it was His Father's will that this man should witness to his town-folk so that they, too, might seek God.

Decapolis was a Gentile area, i.e. a non-Jewish area in Galilee, east of the Jordon River and embracing ten cities. The people who lived there would not have known anything about Jesus or His awesome authority. They needed to be told the good news about Jesus. We read: *"And he departed and began to proclaim in Decapolis all that Jesus had done for him; and all marvelled!" Mark 5:20.*

The work Jesus wanted this man to do was to evangelize - by simply sharing his miracle story or his personal testimony with the people in the area.

We are all different and we all have a special life-time story. Every single born-again believer has a unique personal testimony that God wants us to share with others. To do this, we need to explain three things to others:

(1) What our lives had been like *before* we received Jesus.

(2) When and how we responded to the Gospel message.

(3) What our life has been like *since that time*.

Our personal testimony is a powerful *"spiritual weapon"* to use against Satan, as he tries to deceive other unbelievers. No one can argue with a person's own life story.

For example: You might recall that Jesus had healed a man on the Jewish Sabbath. This man had been blind from birth. Instead of rejoicing that the man had received his sight, the legalistic leaders were offended that Jesus had broken the Sabbath rule by conducting personal ministry on the Jewish holy day. They went to the parents and then to the man himself. He told them his testimony but still the Pharisees said that Jesus was a sinner because He had not kept the Sabbath. Obviously, law-keeping was far more important than a person's sight!

However, the healed man finally said to the Pharisees: *"Whether He is a sinner or not, I do not know; one thing I know: that though I was blind, now I see."* John 9:25. Truth is truth – the Pharisees could not debate any further. His testimony gave them no cause for action.

Back to our story about the demonic man – I believe, like others before me, that his healing was the special mission the Father had given Jesus to do that day, and the miracle of calming the storm was a test that Jesus had deliberately set for His disciples – but fear stopped them from passing that test.

Sometimes, when I experience mental anguish, I think of this lonely man who was an outcast in society. If Jesus set him free, then He can certainly set me free! Most all sicknesses come from a demonic power, while sometimes, we suffer through our own stupidity or by the wrong treatment or actions by others.

What do you think when you read this story? Do you think that Jesus could put an end to your suffering and pain? Would people marvel at your healing? Yes, the people of Decapolis marvelled when they saw this former crazy man in his right mind. Even though I do not consider myself as being crazy, I know that there would be a number of people who would marvel at the healing of my mental disorder.

One important factor - this man didn't seek Jesus! Jesus sought him! Isn't that wonderful! (In saying this, I am not inferring that we are not to seek God for healing – of course He wants us to seek wellness.) Another good thing was that even though this distressed man lived in total isolation, he instantly recognised Jesus as God, deserving worship! But Jesus had crossed over the lake for more than worship - He came to order "Legion" out from the tormented man and to set him free and to give him a brand new life.

- The 3rd and 4th miracles demonstrated that Jesus has authority over sickness, disease and even death itself. These miracles are intertwined and are found in Mark 5:21-43.

[21] *Now when Jesus had crossed over again by boat to the other side, a great multitude gathered to Him; and He was by the*

sea. [22] *And behold, one of the rulers of the synagogue came, Jairus by name. And when he saw Him, he fell at His feet* [23] *and begged Him earnestly, saying, "My little daughter lies at the point of death. Come and lay Your hands on her, that she may be healed, and she will live."* [24] *So Jesus went with him, and a great multitude followed Him and thronged Him.*

[25] *Now a certain woman had a flow of blood for twelve years,* [26] *and had suffered many things from many physicians. She had spent all that she had and was no better, but rather grew worse.* [27] *When she heard about Jesus, she came behind Him in the crowd and touched His garment.* [28] *For she said, "If only I may touch His clothes, I shall be made well."*

[29] *Immediately the fountain of her blood was dried up, and she felt in her body that she was healed of the affliction.* [30] *And Jesus, immediately knowing in Himself that power had gone out of Him, turned around in the crowd and said, "Who touched My clothes?"*

[31] *But His disciples said to Him, "You see the multitude thronging You, and You say, 'Who touched Me?'"*

[32] *And He looked around to see her who had done this thing.* [33] *But the woman, fearing and trembling, knowing what had happened to her, came and fell down before Him and told Him the whole truth.* [34] *And He said to her, "Daughter, your faith has made you well. Go in peace, and be healed of your affliction."*

Imagine having a flow of blood for twelve years and not being able to find healing? Can you imagine spending all your money on doctors to receive healing and them having no answers? You would be in a physically weak state and your emotions would be so sad and desperate.

Jesus had just finished casting out "Legion" and had crossed back to the other side of the water, when he met Jairus, who was one of the rulers of the Jewish synagogue (A Jewish place of worship). Jairus wanted Jesus to heal his daughter who was near death. This faith-filled man knew that if Jesus came to his daughter, she would live.

As the two men were walking, our faith-filled woman with an issue of blood lent forward and touched the hem of the prayer shawl of Jesus. As soon as she touched Jesus' clothes, her blood-flow instantly stopped and she knew she was totally healed. Amazingly, Jesus had sensed power going out from Him to someone and He knew who had been healed. But He wanted the woman of faith, to publically acknowledge her healing.

This reminds me that both faith and confession are needed in salvation. In the same way, both faith and confession are needed in healing.

Paul said: *"If you confess with your mouth the Lord Jesus and believe in your heart that God raised Him from the dead, you will be saved. For with the heart one believes unto righteousness, and with the mouth confession is made unto salvation." Romans 10:9-10.*

Faith followed by confession is a spiritual law of God!

This law can be counted on just like any of God's laws, either spiritual or physical laws. We have the law of gravity, the law of aerodynamics, the law of sowing and reaping, the law of poverty and prosperity, to name a few.

God wants every believer to know that salvation and healing are the twin blessings of the cross of Jesus. King David, who wrote many of the Psalms, linked these two blessings together when he said: *"Bless the Lord, O my soul, and forget not all His benefits; Who forgives all your iniquities, Who heals all your diseases." Psalm 103:2-3.*

Jesus did not rebuke the woman for interrupting His mission to visit the dying girl, but was prepared to delay this mission in order to assure her of healing and salvation. Jesus wanted to perfect the woman's faith and to lead her to a public confession of faith. He rewarded her testimony with the assurance that she could go in peace.

Are we that desperate for a healing? Will we seek out healing like this lady with so much faith? The Jewish law did not allow such a person to even mix with others, so she would have lived an isolated life as an outcast, much like the demon-possessed man had lived. She had spent all her money seeking help and even knowing she was breaking the law, in desperation she reached out in faith to this Jewish Rabbi who had such a wonderful testimony of healing.

Jesus healed many people in the course of a day. Here was a woman who might have given up thinking she would ever be well. I'm sure many of my readers know what I mean. I admit that often, I feel that way myself. I have had very anointed people pray for me and nothing seems to have happened. It's easy to lose hope. And then the Lord reminds me about these stories in the Bible - impossible situations where Jesus miraculously comes through!

When I reflect on these stories, there is a glimmer of hope rising in my heart. When I look at the character of Jesus, there is hope in my heart that "yes," He would like to heal me and set me free.

Jesus is again interrupted - see Mark 5:35-43.

[35] While He was still speaking, some came from the ruler of the synagogue's house who said, "Your daughter is dead. Why trouble the Teacher any further?"[36] As soon as Jesus heard the word that was spoken, He said to the ruler of the synagogue, "Do not be afraid; only believe." [37] And He permitted no one to follow Him except Peter, James, and John the brother of James. [38] Then He came to the house of the ruler of the synagogue, and saw a tumult and those who wept and wailed loudly. [39] When He came in, He said to them, "Why make this commotion and weep? The child is not dead, but sleeping."

[40] And they ridiculed Him. But when He had put them all outside, He took the father and the mother of the child, and those who were with Him, and entered where the child was lying. [41] Then He took the child by the hand, and said to her, "Talitha, cumi," which is translated, "Little girl, I say to you, arise." [42] Immediately the girl arose and walked, for she was twelve years of age. And they were overcome with great amazement. [43] But He commanded them strictly that no one should know it, and said that something should be given her to eat.

Note that Jesus only took His closest disciples into the room where Talitha had died. These men had great faith in their Master. They had witnessed things that the other nine had not been privy to. We can be confident that Jesus knows about our level of faith. He has people who have the gift of healing and He can send them to heal us too. Jesus can give a healer a vision of fore-knowledge concerning us, so that he or she instinctively knows our problem and how to pray for us.

Jesus can give us the faith to go forward, or even cause the healer to call us out from the congregation to come forward and receive healing. God knows all about every one of us.

Getting back to the dead girl: in those days, it was customary to employ professional mourners to display grief at funerals – so when Jesus saw all the people, He said in verse 5:39 *"Why make this commotion and weep? The child is not dead, but sleeping."*

Jesus indicated that it was only a temporary condition! His words were both a rebuke at unbelief and an encouragement to bereaved people then and now. On the cross, Jesus defeated the sting of death for all those who place their faith in Him. We can be assured that when a Christian dies, their soul and their spirit goes immediately to Heaven and all that is left is their empty shell that once housed the real person.

But in the case of twelve year old Talitha, the devil had tried to end her life prematurely, but God had other plans for her. Jesus simply said to her: *"Little girl, I say to you arise,"* and she opened her eyes and was ready to eat.

We might have given up on ourselves, just like the people who had said not to trouble the Teacher anymore. Perhaps, we have been let down by being prayed for in the past and we don't want to trouble another servant of God. After all we assume - we'll just give the healer another failure to experience where his prayers didn't heal.

We can get to a place where we run out of faith for a breakthrough: we can get so worn down. We may say, "Healing works for others but not for me." Perhaps, we hear a personal testimony about healing and it may spark another hurt in us, wishing that it was us. Our hearts are very delicate. We don't want to be considered second class and yet, that is what we feel.

To be honest with you, I don't really mind if I am not healed. I just realize when I wrote those words that maybe, I am just not desperate enough for healing to come. Nevertheless, I have lived for twenty years with my illness and I know as long as I can get medication, I can live for another twenty years or more like this. I guess it's this sort of attitude that does not see me running from church to church that may have special guest speakers who could pray for me.

I kind of think when I read these stories that if Jesus wanted me healed: He would bring a person across my path who knew I was suffering. This person could receive a word of knowledge by the Holy Spirit and without fuss, pray for me and set me free. I guess I just lack that urgent desire because maybe my suffering isn't enough to make me desperate.

I am like that little girl called "Talitha" in one regard - I need to have life brought back into me! It can be very hard to exist in this world with a mental illness and the troubles I go through weigh heavily on me every week. I try to read books on healing to grow my faith for personal healing and yet, I keep putting these books down only partly read.

God has told me through prophecy that one day, I am going to be used powerfully in healing. Most healers I know have been healed first themselves. I guess God has His timing and He knows best as to when I will have the faith to heal others. Perhaps, I might begin to heal others first and when I grow in faith for healing, then my own healing will manifest in my life.

I had wanted to devote this chapter to amazing miracles of Jesus and the story about Legion came to mind. Then I realized the miracle of the storm was first recorded, then the demonic man and finally this last story about the desperate woman and young Talitha. All of them were one after the other – how good is God. The Holy Spirit knew that the stories went in sequence, so He took me by surprise once again.

We know from these stories that healing is possible for all of us. Even if our situation seems impossible - *Jesus could heal us!* In the meantime, every believer is to make the best use of all that God has blessed them with. We are to focus on others and not onto our own problems. But most importantly, we are to plant God's seeds of truth into our hearts, so that we will do the Father's will on earth.

If every time we opened up our Bible, we saw it as literally being hundreds of creative seeds just needing good soil to be planted in, we would sow these seeds into our own heart and we would keep nurturing them until they produced the fruit that God destined for them to grow.

This would be God's will for each of us. I will leave you with that personal challenge.

Chapter 10

Can an Unhealed Person Bring God Glory?

All of us have been created to bring God glory. To read more on the subject, you could read my book called "*Living for eternity*." The invitation to come into salvation, to walk in the Holy Spirit, and to glorify the name of Jesus Christ is open to everyone who believes and responds to the Gospel message.

God definitely didn't create anyone to be a failure! God wants all of us to glorify the name of Jesus Christ by our witness and lifestyle. It is His will that we overcome life's obstacles in the strength of God's Holy Spirit. We need to shine out the love of God, so that others we know and meet will understand that there really is an all-powerful and all knowing, loving God who had done everything He possibly can to draw us into His Own family.

I have a dear friend who truly loves me with the love of Jesus. He has seen a massive change in my life since he first met me. At that particular stage in my life, I was suffering with a sleep disorder which I have already written about. During this eighteen month trial, I was sleeping most days up to eighteen hours every day. However, I would drag myself off to church most weeks and end up weeping throughout the whole service.

My friend, Glen, now sees me as brand new person. He sees me as being very positive, full of joy and being a successful writer. Glen knows that God is very much alive in me and he says that he is happy and proud of the changes that have occurred in my life.

I have had strangers share with me that my books have had a good influence on their life. Therefore, I know that God has been glorified in me. Some people believe that God's anointing is on my books and that inspires me to go on writing. From being a negative person who said I didn't need to be healed in my last chapter, I certainly have a positive side as well.

My positive side is full of joy and encouragement. This attitude often champions others as it brings a light and cheerful atmosphere that we all long for. When I am full of joy and cheer, I am not faking it! I really am feeling that way. I am always honest about how I feel. If I am depressed and suffering with no presence of God in my life, people know about it and when my spirit is up, people know that too.

I guess what is really good though, is that sometimes, when strangers encounter me, even when I am very depressed, they still see a happy person. This is because I have purposely made it a practice to acknowledge people with a smile even when I am depressed. I have discovered that a genuine smile not only picks them up, but it causes a positive change in me.

Do you think that God programmed that into me, despite my own emotional level? I certainly think so – God is so good, all the time. He is good!

Some people are surprised to hear that I suffer with a debilitating mental illness, but even though it's part of me, I refuse to let it define "who" I am.

As a believer, my true identity is "in Christ," therefore, in Him, I am an overcomer because of what Christ achieved for me on the cross. With this thought in mind, I wrote a book called *"Your Identity in Christ"* so that my readers can learn how God sees every believer. He is not looking at any of our imperfections or disabilities, as Father God only sees us through the lens of Jesus Christ, His Son.

The Holy Spirit first prompted me to write about "Your Identity in Christ" and I was continually aware of His prompting as I wrote it. Believers are not to be ignorant of their eternal inheritance. God wants us to know without a doubt that we are a legitimate family member in the Kingdom of God by faith and commitment in the finished work of the cross.

Think about it, how different would your life be, if the Queen of England officially adopted you into her royal family? You would soon discover that you had privileges beyond your wildest dreams. Of course, Her Royal Highness would expect you to act responsibly and not bring dishonor to the throne. In the same way, believers need to be encouraged to continually embrace their "New Birth" privileges. At salvation, every believer is instantly welcomed into the royal household of God as legitimate heirs of God's Kingdom.

Some people have told me that they have read my "identity" book more than once to mine the nuggets of wisdom from it. I feel that in writing it, I have not only glorified the finished work of Jesus and made known the ongoing rippling effect in the lives of believers, but God will be glorified in the hearts of its readers.

Some people may think that an unhealed believer couldn't ever bring glory to God in their current situation. To think that way would be really sad. To believe that lie would mean that people would need to experience perfect health to be used by God and to glorify Him in their life. There are many Christians in the world who are exceptional examples of the love of Jesus by constantly displaying the character of Jesus, yet they remain unhealed.

If God only allowed healed people into His Heaven, it would not reflect His true character. We are told at least three times that I know of that God is an impartial God. To say otherwise, would make the Word of God untrue! God is a good God all the time and His Holy Spirit is powerful and can do great things through anyone who is open to be used by Him. If that was not the case, the following Scripture would not have been written:

"For you see your calling, brethren, that not many wise according to the flesh, not many mighty, not many noble, are called. But God has chosen the foolish things of the world to put to shame the wise, and God has chosen the weak things of the world to put to shame the things which are mighty; and the base things of the world and the things which are despised God has chosen, and the things which are not, to bring to nothing the things that are." 1 Corinthians 1: 26-28.

As a person with Bipolar and Schizophrenia, I can certainly be classified as someone who is one of the "weak" or "foolish" people of the world. Nevertheless, "Praise the Lord" God and the Holy Spirit are not limited in any way because of my health condition. Even in my disability, the Holy Spirit uses me to shine God's light. As a prophet, I might not be always understood, but when I am led to write on certain subjects, I know that many people have had their eyes opened. I am the epitome of the Scripture above.

What about you? Can you be used? Can you shine for Jesus regardless of your pain and suffering? Paul in 1 Corinthians quoted above gives us the confidence that we are indeed qualified to be called by God for great things. There is no partiality with God because He is not a respecter of persons. (Acts 10:34, Romans 2:11 and Galatians 2:6)

"Partiality" refers to those who take sides, showing preference, exhibiting bias or showing discrimination, treating one person better than another. While society makes distinctions among people, God's love and grace are available for all and can be received by anyone.

Believers down through the centuries have held the Apostle Paul in great honor, but that was not always the case. During his lifetime, he knew that he was misunderstood and was seen as being ridiculous by the world's opinion:

"For I think that God has displayed us, the apostles, last, as men condemned to death; for we have been made a spectacle to the world, both to angels and to men. We are fools for Christ's sake, but you are wise in Christ! We are weak, but you are strong! You are distinguished, but we are dishonored! To the present hour we both hunger and thirst and we are poorly clothed, and beaten, and homeless. 1 Corinthians 4: 9-11.

Most people in the West live a pretty good life even though they may suffer. Few of us could claim that we are hungry and thirsty, poorly-clothed and homeless. Very few could say they suffer beatings. You can see by looking at the ministry described here by Paul, that it certainly was not something glamorous.

Preachers today in the West do not suffer these things. They quote Paul, but they did not experience the life that he lived, nor display his great knowledge. Paul says that he was aware that he was seen as a fool in the eyes of some and that he was seen to be weak. I don't think that Paul was suffering from an incurable illness, but he described himself as weak. Today, therefore, even in our weakness, we can still bring glory to God. I am very thankful to God that I am not hungry, thirsty, poorly clothed, beaten or homeless!

Just in case, you are still unconvinced that unhealed people can bring God glory, I want to mention two people whom we can all admire and be encouraged by on YouTube. Both these people have been an awesome inspiration to me and many others.

(1)   Nick Vujicic:

I spoke earlier in chapter six about this incredible man. Look up his name on YouTube and search for the video titled *"Nick Vujicic Look at yourself after watching this."* On the eBook, look at the link https://www.youtube.com/watch?v=Gc4HGQHgeFE and you will see someone who is absolutely remarkable.

Nick was born with no arms or legs. He suffered so much because of this, but gave his heart to Jesus. He has become a highly acclaimed writer and public speaker and goes around the world encouraging people about getting the most out of life. He dreamed of one day being able of have his own wife, and in this video, he had not yet met her, but now, he is married with a child. His life is one of the most inspiring lives I have ever seen and I have read two of his books. One of his books is called *"Life without Limits."* It's really amazing to read such wonderful advice from a person who is exceptionally limited, writing on the subject of "how not to be limited in life!"

If you are reading this book and have not watched the video, maybe you could watch it now as I want to ask you some questions relating to it. How can you look at that video and stay in a pity party? How can you look at Nick's life and not see a brighter future for yourself?

If anyone was destined to be a "poor me," it was Nick. However, God opened doors for him to speak to vast audiences around the world. God encouraged him to enjoy life and do something productive and spectacular for the Kingdom of God. God can do the same for you. God can use all of us to impact others who know Him not and people who feel that they are stunted in life in some way. Nick has proven once and forever that a positive attitude allows God to do exceedingly, abundantly, above all that we ask or think, according to the power that works in us.

I urge you to please take the time to watch his inspiring video. It will greatly encourage those who experience the challenges of life and the constant embarrassment of being physically different from others. Nick is certainly an awesome example of a person who remains unhealed but who brings God amazing glory.

When God has spoken to me about my life and how one day I am going to be preaching around the world, I only have to look at that video to know that God can open doors for anyone. When you feel down and sad, revisit Nick's video on YouTube and catch hold of his exuberance and love of life and listen to his uplifting message for us all. He will certainly inspire you and lift up your spirit.

(2)   Joni Erickson Tada

Joni had an unexpected and horrific accident when swimming one day. She had unknowingly dived into shallow water and broke her spine. For forty-six years since that time, she has lived with constant pain in a wheelchair as a quadriplegic. Like Nick, she is used by God to speak all over the world about her amazing, over-coming Christian faith.

Joni speaks in a video on YouTube about her life called: "Joni Erickson Tada shares her story" In the eBook, you can find it at: https://www.youtube.com/watch?v=VVXJ8GyLgt0. Take the time to watch her inspiring video. It will greatly encourage all those who experience ongoing physical pain and the associated embarrassment regarding the inability to do what others find easy.

Perhaps, you might want to listen to more of Joni and get to know her more. In this video, she speaks of Heaven as giving us little splashes of glory when hell is splashing us with difficulties. Joni hints at the very close and intimate relationship that she has with Jesus. She said that she would never swap her relationship with God even for the ability to walk. Like Nick, Joni is also happily married.

Another short video of Joni on YouTube is called "Joni Erickson Tada on art" and can be found at this link https://www.youtube.com/watch?v=qPi-1QRLPSs.

I have said it before, but I will say it again. My suffering and pain has definitely drawn me very close to Jesus. In fact, at times, I have wondered what my life today would have been like if my family had not had Bipolar in their genepool. You might suffer in a different way, but take the time to get to know Jesus in a closer way. God promises in James that if we draw close to God, He will draw close to us. (James 4:8)

If you have watched both Nick's and Joni's videos, you will certainly realize that God can be glorified in all situations. God wants you to know that He is happy with you and that He loves you. I want you to know that no matter how you are suffering, God still has a way that you can bring glory and honor to His name.

Chapter 11
Can Others be Blessed by Me?

Have you ever been invited to someone's place for a meal and afterwards helped wash the dishes? Some hosts may outwardly protest, but underneath, they are really appreciative of your kindness in such a normally thankless task. Right there and then, you blessed someone.

Have you ever lent a really great book to a friend and they thoroughly enjoyed it and were blessed by it? Once again, you blessed a person.

Have you ever baby-sat for a married couple or for a single mother? Once again, you blessed someone. It's actually quite easy to bless people! All you need to do is take your focus from yourself and put it onto others. When you look at the busy lives of others, sometimes it's quite easy to see ways that you can be a blessing to them.

Unfortunately, some of us are hurting so much that we cannot see past ourselves. Some people suffer so much it takes all their effort to get through a day. In that case, perhaps you can share on Facebook what you are going through. Maybe you could even write a Facebook note or even blog posts about your journey and the things that you are going through. There are many people who are suffering who can be encouraged by your story.

I am a pretty simple person: I don't often use big words. I started work straight after finishing school, so I am not theologically trained. When I write Christian books, much of what I say comes from comments in my King James Bible, which adds weight to what I write. I receive my book titles from the Holy Spirit and He sort of co-writes with me, giving me what to say.

What I am saying is that I am not special, but I am unique. In fact, everyone is unique! I don't think I am anything great, but I am real: meaning I am honest and transparent in what I say and share. People seem to enjoy my writing and God seems to keep picking topics that I have some knowledge about, so as to share with my readers.

If it were up to me, I would find it very hard to come up with subjects to write on. In fact, I know that it would be really hard for me to fill up a book about any topic that I chose. I cannot stress enough how important the Holy Spirit is to me. He is my helper, He is my friend, and He wants to be your friend as well. He helps me; He writes through me; He leads me; He gives me each step to take in my life.

The Holy Spirit wants to help you as well. Do you know the Holy Spirit? Just like He helps me to write books by assisting me to think up the words that I type, so too, the Holy Spirit wants to lead you and give you ideas on how to reach people.

Every one of us has something to offer to make this world a more beautiful place. If you judged the world only by what the media is presenting to you at the present time, you would be so sad. It seems that the world is very dark at the moment. We have to constantly remember that Scripture tells us that persecution and other terrible things will happen in the last days and will get increasingly worse, not better. But as believers, our future security is held firmly in God. God is forever mindful of His Own children:

"Can a woman forget her nursing child, and not have compassion on the son of her womb?

Surely they may forget, yet I will not forget you. See, I have inscribed you on the palm of My hands, your walls are continually before Me." Isaiah 49:15-16.

The words that sustain my mother in times when the devil could play mind games with her is found in Hebrews 12:2a - *"looking unto Jesus, the author and finisher of our faith."* This Holy Spirit advice gives her great assurance that God has all things in hand. Whatever negative things are happening, she knows God's peace within.

As a believer, you have God's Holy Spirit living in you and He has all kinds of wonderful things for you to do. There are heaps of things that you can do with the light of Jesus within you. No matter what you are going through, you have a light within you and you can do good things for God's glory. Jesus told us to never hide our light.

"Nor do they light a lamp and put it under a basket, but on a lampstand, and it gives light to all who are in the house. 16 Let your light so shine before men, that they may see your good works and glorify your Father in heaven." Matthew 5: 15-16.

Jesus and His Holy Spirit have good works for you to do. It only takes a little thought. It's easy to find people who suffer like you. You can join forums online and "Chat" groups and help other people cope with what you are going through. No matter how bad things are for you, there is always someone who is suffering as much or even more than you. They might be feeling very lonely and would love to be befriended and comforted by someone who cares.

Satan wants us to suffer in silence and to give up. He wants us to focus on ourselves and lay down in misery and not help anyone. But Jesus wants us to get our light out, shine it, and encourage people. What are you going to do? A simple thing that you can do that will help others is to write an honest review of this book on Amazon to encourage other people to buy it. You can gift a Kindle copy of this book to a friend who you know would appreciate it.

I urge you not to give up on life. Instead, think of ways you can bless others. Ask God to give you some ideas, for I know that this would be His will for you to do. In fact, I would like to pray for you right now.

Dear Father, You know this reader and the struggles that they are facing. They want to be used to bless other people, so that they can get their mind off their own troubles and also because they want to contribute to others. I ask that through the Holy Spirit you give them a good idea how they can be used to bless others. Make the idea simple, and give them the enthusiasm to reach out to others. I know that you listen to my prayers. I thank you in advance for helping them. In Jesus' name, I ask, amen.

Each of us have things that we can do for others to bless them. Scripture says that we were created to do good works. I will quote a verse first in the New Living Translation and then in the New King James Study Bible.

"For we are God's masterpiece. He has created us anew in Christ Jesus, so we can do the good things he planned for us long ago." Ephesians 2:10. When I think of the word "masterpiece," an exquisite piece of expensive artwork readily comes to mind. However, my Study Bible does not use this word, instead it says:

"For we are His workmanship, created in Christ Jesus for good works, which God prepared beforehand that we should walk in them." Ephesians 2:10.

My King James Study Bible notes give a definition of the word "workmanship" and a rather lengthy explanation about our spiritual "response-ability" concerning human worth and Divine destiny. I have quoted in italic text what my Bible says about this word:

The word "workmanship" is from the verb "poieo," meaning to make. Compare "poem" or "poetry." The word signifies that which is manufactured, a product, a design produced by an artisan. "Poiema" emphasizes God as the Master Designer, the universe as

His creation! "For since the creation of the world His invisible attributes are clearly seen, being understood by the things that are made, even His eternal power and Godhead, so that they are without excuse." Romans 1:20.

Before conversion, our lives had no rhyme or reason. Conversion brought us balance, symmetry, and order. We are God's poem, His work of art. The creature that God created in man is enabled to respond to Him. Man becomes a response-able being. He is, qualitatively, a different sort of being, endowed with ability and a freedom to fellowship and participate in the life of God.

This is not the freedom of individual autonomy, which denies dependence of God. Nor is it the freedom behind the fall of man, as in the case of Adam and Eve (Genesis 3.) Adam and Eve were given the freedom to respond to God following their disobedience, but instead attempted to hide from Him. Sin is the disobedience that severs man's fellowship with God. Sin confuses and distorts our humanity and obstructs the emergence of a true person-hood by interrupting our fellowship with God.

But when the power of sin is broken – by accepting Christ's vicarious act of obedience at Calvary – grace is revealed and the true order of humanity is restored. It is in the crucified humanity of Jesus that we find the true humanity originally intended in creation. Christ came to authenticate humanity in order for us to be in full communion with God.

These truths are summarized by the apostle Paul who says that by nature, the human condition of mankind is dead, enslaved, and condemned. (Ephesians 2:1-3); but then, by the grace of God in

Christ and His divine compassion, man is saved, made alive (Ephesians 2:5, and 8), raised, and made to sit with Him in eternal fellowship and purpose (Ephesians 6-10)

The genius of God's new creation work in each believer is that He renovates the nature of His redeemed children to make "good works" a living possibility. Therefore, what are the good works that you were designed to do? Are you already doing them? God wants you to be a blessing to others. Please write to me and tell me what you have decided to do.

Chapter 12
What Was Paul's Thorn in the Flesh?

We read in 2 Corinthians 12:1-10 below that Paul had been graciously and miraculously caught up into Paradise, and so that he would not be tempted to exalt himself above measure by boasting of his privileged experience, a messenger from Satan caused a "thorn" in Paul's flesh. Despite his pleas to the Lord to remove this thorn, God chose not to do this for him, because He wanted Paul to depend on His goodness alone, and not be swayed by physical circumstances. Let's review this story:

"It is doubtless not profitable for me to boast. I will come to visions and revelations of the Lord: I know a man in Christ who fourteen years ago—whether in the body I do not know, or whether out of the body I do not know, God knows—such a one was caught up to the third heaven. And I know such a man—whether in the body or out of the body I do not know, God knows— how he was caught up into Paradise and heard inexpressible words, which it is not lawful for a man to utter. Of such a one I will boast; yet of myself I will not boast, except in my infirmities. For though I might desire to boast, I will not be a fool; for I will speak the truth. But I refrain, lest anyone should think of me above what he sees me to be or hears from me. 2 Corinthians 12:1-6.

Verse 7 - *And lest I should be exalted above measure by the abundance of the revelations, a thorn in the flesh was given to me, a messenger of Satan to buffet me, lest I be exalted above measure. Concerning this thing I pleaded with the Lord three times that it might depart from me. And He said to me, "My grace is sufficient for you, for My strength is made perfect in weakness." Therefore most gladly I will rather boast in my infirmities, that the power of Christ may rest upon me. Therefore I take pleasure in infirmities, in reproaches, in needs, in persecutions, in distresses, for Christ's sake. For when I am weak, then I am strong. 2 Corinthians 12:7-10.*

Of course a thorn in the natural is like a fine, sharp splinter which of course can be easily removed, but what was Paul's thorn? Scripture tells us the answer – it was "a messenger of Satan."

What do other Bibles say this thorn was? The Amplified, the Revised Standard, The New Schofield Reference, the New International Version, The New American Standard, all agree with my King James New Spirit Filled Life Bible, that it was a messenger of Satan. Only the Living New Testament Bible, which is really only a Paraphrase Bible, says it was a sickness.

Therefore, out of the seven different translations which I have, only the Living New Testament Paraphrase Bible said it was a sickness. Therefore, I would confidently conclude that Paul's "thorn" was indeed a messenger of Satan who was sent by this demonic being to stir up trouble in Paul's personal life so that it could ultimately affect his rapidly expanding ministry. The plan: destroy Paul, then the radical teaching he was preaching would cease! A messenger is always a "personality" and in Paul's case, this messenger had been given a specific assignment: to buffet Paul!

My Concise Oxford dictionary says that "the word "buffet" means: strike with; blow of the hand; knock; hurt; plague; contend with; beating; repeated blows." This is consistent to the buffeting Paul experienced in his various trials and tribulations. (The word "buffet" can also refer to 'irregular oscillation caused by air eddies, of any part of an aircraft' according to my dictionary.

When I was a young Christian, I can remember being told that the New Testament reveals the Old Testament. At the time of the Old Testament, the New Testament truths were concealed, for they had not yet been written. Over the years, I realized that in order to understand the New Testament, I needed to have a basic knowledge of the Old Testament. For its only when we link them up together that we can see the amazing story of God's dealings with man from the very beginning to the very end.

Therefore, we are to view the whole Bible as being like a huge jigsaw puzzle. When all its pieces are put together in the correct spot, we can see a clear picture, but if some pieces are missing, then the true picture is obviously somewhat a mystery.

For example: When God gave Moses His instructions for the conquest of Canaan, He warned him to do a complete job in destroying "all" the Canaanites, *"But if you do not drive out the inhabitants of the land from before you, then it shall be that those whom you let remain shall be irritants in your eyes and* **thorns** *in your sides, and they shall harass you in the land where you dwell." Numbers 33:55* (Emphasis mine.)

Much later, after Moses had died and Joshua was actually preparing to finish up his leadership, he gathered his leaders together for a farewell address. Some of them had chased after foreign gods and the Lord was angry with them. Among other things, he refers to the heathen nations of Canaan and tells his people: *"know for certain that the Lord your God will no longer drive out these nations from before you. But they shall be snares and traps to you, and scourges on your sides and* **thorns** *in your eyes, until you perish from this good land which the Lord you God has given you." Joshua 23:13.* (Emphasis mine.)

As I have said before in Chapter 9, demons are evil spirits who hate being disembodied, so they seek out available physical bodies to work through. The word "thorns" in Scripture refer to wicked spiritual personalities who are evil messengers of the devil sent to harass and buffet those who were originally created in God's image and whom Christ died for.

However, some people are still adamant that Paul's thorn in the flesh was a form of sickness or disability. These people therefore feel justified in having a sickness that won't leave them.

Let's be rational: A fallen angel of the devil could definitely cause another human to beat up someone with many blows, but any "form of sickness" couldn't possibly do that.

Before Saul was renamed Paul, Ananias, through a vision from the Lord, was told to heal Saul's eyes. They had been blinded by the radiant glory of the Risen Lord. Ananias was at first fearful because of Saul's hatred and violence towards believers so Jesus reassured him: *"Go, for he is a chosen vessel of Mine to bear My name before Gentiles, kings, and the children of Israel. For I will show him how many things he must suffer for My name's sake." Acts 9:15-16.*

Ananias went to Paul's house and prayed for him to receive back his sight. *"Immediately there fell from his eyes something like scales, and he received his sight at once; and he rose and was baptized." Revelations 9:18.*

The Book of Acts records many of the trials and tribulations Paul suffered for Christ:

- Jews wanted to kill him after his conversion. 9:23
- He was at first hindered in joining the Christians. 9:26
- He was opposed by a sorcerer. 13:6-12, and by Jews in a mob. 13:50
- He was expelled out of Iconium. 14:1-6
- He was left for dead after stoning. 14:8 and19
- He was beaten and jailed at Philippi. 16:12 and 16-40

- He was disputing with false brethren in Thessalonica and was expelled. 17:1-10

  - He was mobbed & expelled from Berea. 17:10-14

  - He was opposed and sworn at in Macedonia. 18:6

  - There was a plot against his life by the Jews. 20:3

He was seized by Jews, mobbed, tried in court 5 times and suffered other hardships.

He lists buffetings in 2 Corinthians 6:5-10 – stripes, imprisonments, tumults, dishonor, evil report, deceivers, as dying, and behold, we live, as chastened, and not killed. The words dying and living, chastened and not killed are based on Psalm 118:17-18, which actually refer to the Lord Jesus. Some of Paul's hardships were imposed by others, while some were the results of disciplines freely chosen for the sake of the ministry.

In 2 Corinthians 11:22-24, Paul mentions stripes above measure, in prisons more frequent, in deaths often. He also says: *"Of the Jews 5 times received I thirty-nine stripes. Three times I was beaten with rods, once I was stoned, 3 times I suffered shipwreck, a night and a day in the deep, in perils of waters, in perils of robbers, in perils by my own countrymen, in perils by the heathen, in perils in the city, in perils in the wilderness, in perils in the sea, in perils among false brethren; in weariness and painfulness, in hunger and thirst, in cold and nakedness."* 2 Corinthians 11:24-27.

The point I am trying to stress is that the Bible says nothing about Paul being sick! Yet, people have suffered needlessly for years, believing it was God's will for them to be sick because of our opening passage about Paul's thorn in the flesh.

Why then was Satan's messenger sent to buffet Paul? God knew that Paul did not want to fall into boasting about the incredible revelations that he had received when he had been caught up into Paradise in a vision. He said *"Lest I should be exalted above measure through the abundance of the revelations."* 2 Corinthians 12:7.

If you haven't experienced the wonderful revelations that Paul experienced whilst in Paradise, then you should certainly not claim a "thorn" like Paul, for yourself. If you think that God allowed Satan to give you your sickness, then glorify that sickness and don't do anything to get rid of it or seek relief from it in any way.

I personally feel that the thorn was a demon that came upon people wherever Paul went, with one agenda: to stir up trouble for him.

The demon would have hated Paul's message of love and redemption, just as much as all demons hate it today. The agenda of the demonic world is to stamp out Christianity because it's all about God's Son rescuing us from Satan's grip.

Paul, being a man of keen discernment, could see that this was happening and hampering his ministry efforts as well as getting him beaten up and hurt by people, so he asked the Lord three times to stop this from happening. The Lord replied to Him, *"My grace is sufficient for you, for My strength is made perfect in weakness."* 2 Corinthians 12:9.

We can take the Lord's words to Paul and apply them to ourselves. *"My strength is made perfect in weakness,"* While we are suffering and having a hard time, we can still do good works. Whilst we suffer, we can call on the power of the Holy Spirit to help us. Even in the midst of hard times, we can do something great and glorify the name and the power of God.

For the last year, on my weekends and my days off from serving coffee, I have fallen back into a bad sleep pattern. However, this week, as I write this book, I have been getting up at a reasonable time because of my inner motivation to finish this book.

Because I know that it is the Holy Spirit in me, compelling me to keep writing, I see that His strength is made perfect in my weaknesses. When we are weak and suffering, the Holy Spirit can empower us and people can be shocked at us doing something that is normally impossible for us. Yes, people notice the difference when the Holy Spirit empowers us.

Paul had come to the place of contentment in just being in Christ. He says:

"Therefore I take pleasure in infirmities, in reproaches, in needs, in persecutions, in distresses, for Christ's sake. For when I

am weak, then I am strong. 2 Corinthians 12:10.

In Scripture, the word "weakness" is contrasted with power or strength. It doesn't ever convey the idea of weakness as being a sickness or disease. Paul had a great attitude. He obviously suffered far more than most of us today, yet he says that he took pleasure in these things.

I previously said that we need to look at what Christ went through to feel better and promote hope in our life, but we can add Paul's trials to that of the trials that Jesus experienced. Paul suffered so much, yet he said that when he was weak, that was the very time he was strong.

When we are weak and are at the end of ourselves, this is when the Holy Spirit carries us. In saying that, I am reminded of the well-known illustration of the "footsteps in the sand," where a person asks Jesus why He was not with them during their major trials in life. Jesus replied: "My Son, it was during those days that I had to carry you!"

Paul knew that the people causing him trouble would see for themselves how he persisted in his beliefs despite what they did to him. I certainly believe that preachers in China who are flung into prison for having illegal churches bring God much glory.

Getting up and blessing people is a way that you and I can give God glory. I know that I am doing my best, and I know beyond doubt that even being up now is a work of the Holy Spirit and nothing of me.

Finally, Paul's thorn in the flesh never stopped his ministry because he said: *"For I am the least of the apostles, who am not worthy to be called an apostle, because I persecuted the church of God. But by the grace of God I am what I am, and His grace toward me was not in vain; but I laboured more abundantly than they all, yet not I, but the grace of God which was with me."* 1Corinthians 15:9-10.

Did Saul persecute the church of God? Yes! In the verse above, Paul admits he persecuted the church of God. He knew what he was like before being converted and before he received his new name from Jesus. The former "Saul" had been a zealous Pharisee who thought he was doing God a favor by trying to stamp out the rapidly growing numbers of believers in Christ. He saw them as a threat to his precious Judaism!

He had said of himself: *"As for Saul, he made havoc of the church, entering every house, and dragging off men and women, committing them to prison."* Acts 8:3.

However, God had seen his zeal for protecting truth as he saw it! So even though his theology was wrong, his heart was right and God is more concerned about out heart than anything else! His forthright passion for God and his brilliant knowledge of the Old Testament caused God to make this man to be the spiritual father of the Christian Church. (God had found His spokesperson – he had just needed to be converted so that this former activist for truth - was actually discerning it correctly!)

Getting back to the thorn in Paul's flesh, Paul claimed that he had labored more abundantly than anyone else in 1 Corinthians 15:10 above. Ask yourself this question: How could a sick man labor more abundantly than those who were well?

If the statement, "My grace is sufficient for you," meant that God was telling Paul to keep his sickness, it would be the only case in the Bible where God told a person He wanted them to remain sick: that He would give them grace for a physically sick body.

Why would I consider this to be unreasonable? Because the grace of God is imparted only to the *"inner"* person, which Paul says was *renewed every day*.

"Therefore, we do not lose heart. Even though our outward man is perishing, yet the inward man is being renewed day by day. For our light affliction, which is but for a moment, is working for us a far more exceeding and eternal weight of glory, while we do not look at the things which are seen, but at the things which are not seen. For the things which are seen are temporary, but the things which are not seen are eternal. 2 Corinth Corinthians 4:16-18.

Paul knew that our "attitude" towards trials in life is the acid test of every believer.

My Bible notes say: As Paul endured hardships and surrendered himself to the possibility of death, he was in fact, following the pattern of Jesus. However, in the *midst of his perils*, he could experience the "life" of Jesus, strengthening and sustaining him in his present weakness and assuring him of future resurrection.

Paul had been saying earlier: *"For we who live are always delivered to death for Jesus' sake, that the life of Jesus also may be manifested in our mortal flesh."* 2 Corinthians 4:11.

My Bible notes continue: God's grace renews our soul, but the overcoming life of Jesus is manifested in our mortal flesh. This means that the providential hand of God was controlling Paul's persecutions, keeping them within manageable proportions."

Can you, in God's strength, remain strong for God?

Chapter 13

Does God Love Me Less Than Others?

When you are suffering and in pain, you sometimes get the thought that God doesn't love you like He loves other people. If that thought ever comes to you, *I want you to rebuke it in the Name of Jesus!* Such a thought is contrary to the Word of God. It actually comes from the pit of hell – meaning it comes from demons. Yet, this type of thinking that we are not loved like others seems to be true to many of us who suffer. We are led to think that we are somehow less fortunate, somehow less loved by God because He allows us to be sick and to suffer.

At this stage, it's important that you realize that there are different types of love:

The first time we see the word, "love as showing affection for someone" is in Genesis where God speaks to Abraham, *"Then He said, 'Take now your son, your only son Isaac, whom you love and go to the land of Moriah, and offer him there as a burnt offering on one of the mountains of which I shall tell you.'"* Genesis 22:2.

My Bible notes confirm that an "only son" is indeed a precious life. In Abraham's case, it referred to his miracle child, Isaac, born to his once barren wife, Sarah, who was about ninety years old at the time. The place where God told Abraham to sacrifice his precious son is the same place where God sacrificed His *"Own precious Son"* in the hills of Moriah, in Jerusalem. Equally noteworthy is that the phrase *"His only begotten Son"* as used in John 3:16 – this Scripture is the most quoted in the whole of the Bible because it sums up the Gospel message in a brief and simple way.

God's type of love is virtually unknown to people who are not familiar with the New Testament. God's kind of love doesn't need chemistry, or affinity, or a feeling. *Agape love* such as this belongs exclusively to the Christian community, but God wants the whole world to know about it experientially.

A "burnt offering" was the most common sacrifice of all the Jewish sacrifices to God. It foreshadowed Jesus Christ, the true Burnt Sacrifice, who alone makes us acceptable by God.

It is not clear why God chose a potential "human sacrifice" as Abraham's test as He clearly forbids such a practice in Deuteronomy 18:10. The main point is obviously the test of faith, for God ended up providing a lamb for Abraham to sacrifice once Abraham's faith had been severely tested.

Another kind of love is called *"ahab"* and this means to have "affection" for someone, perhaps a close friend. It can sometimes refer to (1) loving the Lord and (2) hating evil as in Psalm 97:10 which says: "You who love the Lord, hate evil!" It can even refer to an idea, or a pleasure etc.

Another kind of love is called *"phileo"* love. You will recall the time when Peter had betrayed Jesus by cowardly saying he didn't know Him. Later, after the resurrection, Jesus questioned Peter's love three times. Peter replied in John 21:15 *"Yes, lord; You know that I love You."* Jesus had asked Peter three times if he had *"agape"* love. Peter answered with *"phileo,"* which at that moment was all he had to give. His love meant he was fond of, cared for affectionately, cherished, took pleasure in, have personal attachment for – much like the love between a husband and a wife.

Later, when the Holy Spirit imparted to Peter the fuller understanding of God's kind of love (*agape*) Peter knew the difference. *"Agape"* is the highest form of love and is used by Paul: *"Now hope does not disappoint, because the love of God has been poured out in our hearts by the Holy Spirit who was given to us."* Romans 5:5.

We can only experience this high form of love by the power of the Holy Spirit. *Agape* love is unconditional goodwill that seeks the highest good of another person, no matter what he does. It is the self-giving love that gives freely without asking anything in return, and does not consider the personal worth of its object.

Agape is more a love by choice than *Phileo*, which is love by chance, and it refers to the will, rather than the emotion. We love God and others because "we will" to love them that way. *Agape* describes the unconditional love God has for the world - *"For God so loved the world that He gave His only Son, that whoever believes in Him should not perish but have everlasting life." John 3:16.*

I want to share with you a very strange event that happened in my life. Thirteen years ago, I heard Jesus in my dream tell me to contact Jonathan Edwards, the medium. I asked Jesus in my dream: "How can I do that?" He told me just to say his name. So I said, "Jonathan Edwards." As soon as I said it, he replied.

"Hello, this is Jonathan, who am I speaking to?"

"This is Matthew Payne. I am not dead but alive."

"What is your message?" he said in a very formal business-like manner.

"Jesus told me to contact you. He wants you to stop being a Medium. Do you know Jesus?"

"Yes, okay, is that your message?" Jonathan asked.

"Yes that's it."

"Okay, bye."

When he said bye, I woke up totally shocked. I asked Jesus. "Did that really happen?"

'Yes, it did, Matthew." Jesus replied.

"Why did I give him the message?"

'Someone had to give him the message. I chose you. Now, I want you to ask me for something. I have noticed that whenever you speak to me, you never ask me for anything. I want you to ask me for something now and I will grant your request" Jesus said.

"What should I ask you for?' I asked.

"You think about it. Make it something good."

As soon as I thought, I remembered the passage in Acts that quotes Joel the prophet about men seeing dreams and people having visions. I asked, "Jesus I want to see visions and have prophetic dreams."

"Okay!" he said.

Two weeks later, I had my first vision of Jesus. I started to meet Jesus often. One time, I asked Jesus if He could bring people from Heaven down for me to meet and He did. He brought another saint from Heaven for me to talk to. From that time, I have seen and talked to Jesus hundreds of times. I have been to Heaven and have seen my mansion up there and other lovely things. I have spoken about these heavenly trips in my other books.

When I share my supernatural encounters in depth, people often become jealous of me. I think that perhaps the wrong spirit tells them that God loves me more than them. But I know that God just answered my request for the supernatural, because He told me He would.

So I ask you - does God love me more or does he love me less than others?

My reply is emphatically "No!" The question is an invalid question, because God loves every person equally. We can't put Almighty God in a human box – we love people by the way they love us. God is so different – He is so more mature; His love is so deeper and higher than ours. He only knows the highest form of love – *and that's agape love!*

Even though I suffer with mental illness, I am very conscious that I enjoy a different sort of relationship with God to that of some of my friends. I certainly would not advise anyone to contact a medium so that they could have visions. Moses told us very clearly in the Old Testament not to do such a thing. We are to avoid wicked customs - see Deuteronomy 18.

God's Word tells us in verses Deuteronomy 18: 14-15 - *"but as for you, the Lord your God has not appointed such for you. The Lord your God will raise up for you a Prophet* (This being Jesus) *like me from your midst, from your brethren. Him you shall hear."*

Maybe I was unwise to contact Jonathon through telepathy, but I certainly do not subscribe to the lie that God loves me either less or more than other people. *There is no partiality with God*, and with that, I am content. God knew that the devil would play mind games with us concerning His love, so He gave us multiple verses to dispel the devil's lie.

1. Peter said: *"In truth I perceive that God shows no partiality." Acts 10: 34b*

2. Paul said: *"For there is no partiality with God." Romans 2: 10*

3. Peter said: *"In truth I perceive that God shows no partiality." Acts 10:34b*

4. Paul said: *"God shows personal favoritism to no man." Galatians 2:6b*

Are you convinced? God has no favorites! When we are assaulted with thoughts that God loves others who are not suffering more than us, we must dismiss it as a deliberate and hurtful lie from the enemy.

There are so many of us who are hurting and all of us want to be healed and set free! This is true. However, we need to know that God loves us, He, in fact, adores us. We are afflicted by the power of Satan who is playing mind games in our head about suffering and disease.

Oh yes, other Christians who speak of healing and try to heal people might give up on us and say that we have no faith, because their prayers won't work on us. But I say it again. We are not less than others and *God does not love us less!*

Chapter 14

How Do I Get the Faith to be Healed?

In Chapter 9, I wrote about the demonic man who had a legion of evil spirits squatting in his body, which caused him to be a violent and lonely outcast. This wretched man didn't have the intellect or the opportunity to seek Jesus, but Jesus was led by His Father to seek him and to heal him, so that he could become a witness to the goodness of God to all he met. God is always able to sovereignly work in people, according to His purposes.

In the same chapter, we were reminded that even the wind and waves are subject to the mighty voice of Jesus. He had calmed the raging storm with just three words before setting the possessed man free.

I now want to talk about a miracle that the apostle Peter performed by using the powerful Name of Jesus. But first, I want to share what a lady named Lydia Baxter knew about this wonderful Name. Lydia suffered severe health problems but she told her friends: "Jesus is a Comforting Name and He has given me special armor: I have the Name of Jesus to call on! When the tempter tries to make me blue or despondent, I mention His Name, and he can't get through to me anymore"

With this attitude Lydia wrote a wonderful old song:

> *Take the Name of Jesus with you,*
> *Child of sorrow and of woe;*
> *It will joy and comfort give you,*
> *Take it then where're you go.*
>
> *Precious Name! Oh, how sweet!*
> *Hope of earth and joy of Heav'n*
> *Precious Name! Oh, how sweet!*
> *Hope of earth and Joy of Heav'n*

At His voice, someday graves are going to split wide open and the physical dead bodies of all believers are going to be instantly reunited with their heavenly spirit and soul. Then, we who are alive on earth will be instantly gathered up in the air with the Lord to be with Him forever. Therefore comfort one another with this promise. Read Thessalonians 4:15-17.

At the Name of Jesus, not only are sins forgiven but God has promised us: *"their sins and their lawless deeds, I will remember no more." Hebrews 12:17.* Unlike God, we may forgive the sins of others, but our memory of them does not go away.

Now, to my story: A man who had been born lame was instantly healed by the Name of Jesus!

"Now Peter and John went up together to the temple at the hour of prayer, the ninth hour. And a certain man lame from his mother's womb was carried, whom they laid daily at the gate of the temple which is called Beautiful, to ask alms from those who entered the temple; who, seeing Peter and John about to go into the temple, asked for alms. And fixing his eyes on him, with John, Peter said, "Look at us." So he gave them his attention, expecting to receive something from them. Acts 3:1-5.

The ninth hour on the Jewish clock would be about three o'clock mid-afternoon, as the Jewish day commences at six o'clock our time in the morning. This day began no different than any other Sabbath. Many Jews had to pass by this beggar in order to worship the Lord. This man didn't ask Peter for a miracle, he was only interested in begging for change. He was probably at the gate when Jesus walked through, yet he had never asked Him to heal him either. He certainly didn't expect this day to be different to any other Sabbath.

But this particular day was God's day for him to be healed!

"Then Peter said, "Silver and gold I do not have, but what I do have I give you: In the name of Jesus Christ of Nazareth, rise up and walk." And he took him by the right hand and lifted him up, and immediately his feet and ankle bones received strength. So he, leaping up, stood and walked and entered the temple with them -

walking, leaping, and praising God. And all the people saw him walking and praising God. Then they knew that it was he who sat begging alms at the Beautiful Gate of the temple; and they were filled with wonder and amazement at what had happened to him." Acts 3:6-10.

This is more than an interesting story with a happy ending. The story tells us that there is not only healing power in Jesus Himself, but there is healing power in the very "Name" of Jesus! Peter and John were both astonished and overjoyed by the miracle that occurred. Having no money, they had given the man the only thing they had to offer. Peter simply gave what he had: he spoke in the miracle working authority of the Name of Jesus!

Two thousand years later, believers across the world still have this same authority to use the Name of Jesus.

When the people saw this former lame beggar leaping and praising God, the rulers and elders of Israel questioned Peter who instantly and boldly gave glory to where it was due:

"Let it be known to you all, and to all the people of Israel, that by the name of Jesus Christ of Nazareth, whom you crucified, whom God raised from the dead, by Him this man stands here before you whole. This is the stone which was rejected by you builders, which has become the chief cornerstone. Nor is there salvation in any other for there is no other name under heaven given among men by which we must be saved." Acts 4:12.

The rulers and elders were speechless! What could they say? The healing miracle was clearly evident to all the people. They knew they had a problem that needed to be solved: the people could follow Jesus and not them! They tried threatening the disciples, but it didn't work.

The healed man had probably been begging for money for about forty years and now he was flamboyantly dancing, and the people were delighted.

However, at some time, the healed man would have to consider the financial consequences of his miracle. Being healed was exciting and wonderful, but now he could no longer beg for money. He would need to search for some kind of paid work in order to survive and he certainly wasn't trained for anything except begging.

Some of us, maybe even me included, may have conflicting thoughts when it comes to personal healing. Let me be honest, those who are currently on disability pensions would need to find employment if they were miraculously healed, and they would lose most of their free time to do whatever they wanted. I confess that this reality has been a problem to me. Of course, if you were on an age-pension, it would not make much difference. But I am not old enough to be eligible for an age pension, so I would need to get employment.

I would therefore, need to resolve in my heart not to let fear or intimidation ruin my chances of finding suitable employment. I would need to confidently trust God that He would finish completely the good work He has started in me. Even now, this verse comes to mind: *"being confident of this very thing, that He who has begun a good work in you will complete it until the day of Jesus Christ." Philippians 1:6.*

My rational mind tells me that if God is powerful enough to heal people, then He certainly is resourceful enough to help them find work. I know that Roger Sapp, a writer and healer, has met people who are aware of the employment dilemma associated with healing and he often has to first counsel people before they can be healed. Roger has written an exciting book on the subject of healing called *Spiritual Treasure*.

The more we realize that healing is God's will for us, the more likely we will be healed when an anointed person prays and lays hands on us for healing. It is so important to know that Jesus healed every person that came to him. He didn't fail once. Although when the blind man at Bethsaida was healed in Mark 8:22-26, Jesus had to make two attempts before the full healing occurred.

Something to ponder: At the end of the above story in Mark 8:26, Jesus requested that the once blind man was not to tell anyone what had happened. This request of silence was given to the family of Talitha, who was raised from the dead in Mark 5:43 and it was also given by Jesus when He cleansed a leper in Matthew 8:4. Why did Jesus want silence?

My Bible notes teach: "A great outburst of excitement may interfere with the teaching ministry of Jesus which could precipitate a crisis before His ministry was completed."

"So then faith comes by hearing, and hearing by the word of God." Romans 10:17.

Jesus never wanted His miracles to have more prominence than His teaching. It's only by hearing the Word of God that develops saving faith, not the excitement and exuberance of miracles. We would all delight in seeing miracles. But not all of us are anxious to hear the Word of God, are we?

And Jesus went about all Galilee, teaching in their synagogues, preaching the gospel of the kingdom, and healing all kinds of sickness and all kinds of disease among the people. Then His fame went throughout all Syria; and they brought to Him all sick people who were afflicted with various diseases and torments, and those who were demon-possessed, epileptics, and paralytics; and He healed them. Great multitudes followed Him—from Galilee, and from Decapolis, Jerusalem, Judea, and beyond the Jordan. Matthew 4: 23-25.

Jesus was amazing when He walked on earth and He is still just as amazing today. Some of us may have been prayed for many times, yet we still need to be healed! I personally feel that in my case, the prospect of losing my disability pension may be a major factor. Satan thrives on giving us fear because he doesn't want us well or enjoying life.

Suffering for year after year is bad enough, but it's made worse when many well-meaning people pray for you and then get upset when you aren't healed. It's one thing being sick, but quite another thing to feel guilty because someone's prayer had failed. I have found that some Christians can be very negative, especially when their prayers are not answered. They seem more upset about their prayer failure than about the person who is desperate for healing.

Even though I have met Jesus many times in visions, I have never once asked Him to lay hands on me and to heal me. Actually, He would only need to say to me: "be healed!" After all, He only used three words, "peace be still" to calm the sea and the wind! I often ponder that. I guess it might be that Roger Sapp is right! I have been accustomed to having easy money with no strings and I am just too lazy or too fearful to change my circumstances. Doing voluntary work two days a week is fine by me.

Are you in the same position? Do you get your identity out of being the suffering, sick one? Would you lose your identity if you were healed? Strictly speaking, our real identity has nothing to do with sickness or employment. Our true identity is being hidden "in Christ" and when we truly walk in that identity, other things will take a back seat.

Having said all that, I can see myself actually being healed one day! I know that the more I read about healing, the more faith and the less fear I will have on the subject. It certainly won't hurt to study up on the whole subject of healing. I know that many of you would have already researched the subject and are still praying for healing. All I can do is to encourage you not to give up on life or in your prayers.

Roger has written a number of books and has personally healed about 25,000 people. I think reading his books would be very helpful. The thing is, every time I pick up his book *Performing Miracles and Healing* I tend to only read a little bit and then put it down again, I guess I really need to get to a point where I am sick and tired of being sick! Then, God may cause me to become the person He wants me to be.

The important thing for us to accept and to understand is that we are not less loved by God nor are we less valuable in His sight. Even in suffering, we can make an effort to be kind-hearted and generous to others and be a blessing to them and thereby, bring glory to God.

The Holy Spirit gave me the chapter title, but I feel ill-equipped with the subject matter as I feel that I haven't yet really discovered my own answers to the problem.

Chapter 15
I Am Loved Without Cause

I know that I am loved by Jesus. Not only does He tell me personally, but He tells me though prophetic words. There is nothing we have done to deserve this love, yet He chooses to lavish His love on us!

Before we were made righteous, Jesus died for us.

"For when we were still without strength, in due time Christ died for the ungodly. For scarcely for a righteous man will one die; yet perhaps for a good man someone would even dare to die. But God demonstrates His own love toward us, in that while we were still sinners, Christ died for us. Romans 5:6-8.

This is such a comforting Scripture for me. Though I suffer, I know that Jesus suffered exceedingly far, far, more in order to wash me free of my sins.

Jesus chose to leave Heaven and live a misunderstood life on earth and then die a horrific death for me and for you. He did not back down from his coming crucifixion. At any time, He could have. He could have called down thousands of willing angels to rescue Him, but He went forward with His Father's will.

Just thinking about His death makes me pause. It was such a sacrificial love that He had purposed in His heart not only for me, but for the whole world. Surely, we are all loved without cause.

There is nothing that is good enough about me that caused me to be saved! It was purely the will of God that I was chosen to be justified even before I was born. God is amazing. I celebrate the fact that I know God and that He loves me. It might take a few years before I am healed, or it may not even happen, but the fact remains that Jesus saw to it that I was saved and brought me into fellowship with Him. Knowing Jesus and sharing with Him as a much loved friend is so rewarding to me. The more I suffer, the more I hold onto the love I have for Jesus. His love for me sustains me in the worst times and in the good days.

I was having trouble getting to sleep last night and while I was becoming frustrated, Jesus told me He was there with me. It is not enough for Him just to be my Savior in Heaven, but He wants to be my friend in bed with me as I struggle trying to get to sleep.

I want you to know that Jesus doesn't want to be someone that you know in theory; He wants to be with you every step that you take in life. He doesn't want to just be the spiritual focus of your life. Jesus wants to be invited to be actively involved in every area of your life. He wants to help you cope with life, moment by moment. He wants to be with you all day, every day, even if you suffer without reprieve, Jesus wants you to know how precious you are.

How do I know this?

I know this because He wants to be with me and I'm no one special in this world. I know that if He wants to be with me throughout my life, then He wants to be with you!

Some of my readers may have never invited Jesus into their heart to be their Savior. You might be reading this book with an open mind, and gleaning what you can from it. I want you to know that you can personally come to know Jesus very easily. Simply invite Him into your life to be your Savior by saying the following prayer:

Dear God in Heaven, I would love to know Jesus and have Him as a friend in my life. I acknowledge that I have done bad things, and I ask that you would forgive me for them. I ask that Jesus might come and live within my heart through His Spirit. I believe that Jesus died on the cross and rose on the third day, in order to make a way for my sins to be forgiven and pave the way for my new life in Him. I ask that Jesus might be with me from this day on as I try to obey Him in what He taught. Come Lord Jesus. Come into my heart right now. In Jesus name I pray these things. Amen.

If you have prayed that prayer for the first time, please get in touch with a Christian that you know and tell them that you have become a Christian. You might have a relative or friend that you think might be praying for you. Let them know you prayed that prayer and ask them to help you with your Christian faith from now on.

If the people are too far away to meet in person, ask God to lead you to the church He has in mind for you. Tell the pastor you prayed that prayer and that you want to learn more about the Christian faith and ask him if there is someone in the church to teach you more about your new life in Jesus. (This is so important to do. Otherwise, the devil will try to tell you that it's a waste of time and he will try to tell you that you are just being emotional.)

I know personally that I am loved without cause. I know that God and His Son Jesus are very proud of me and love me with an extravagant love. I want every one of my readers to know that they are precious in God's sight: they are loved equally as much as people who are whole, and who have no suffering in their life.

I love you, too. Yes, God has done a new thing in my life as I have written this book and I knew He would. But I wrote this book for all the hurting people who will either buy it or download it. I really want to encourage you to look to Jesus and be reassured of His deep love for you. Your life is precious to Him and He wants you to live it to the full.

Though you may feel insignificant or weak, I want you to know that you have much potential and God has a great purpose for you in life. If I could somehow stop your suffering and pain, you know that I would. In the meantime, I send you my love and spiritually hold hands with you and bless you.

It is my prayer that you know that you are important and greatly loved by God. It's my prayer that you know you can be used to bring God glory just the way that you are. It is my prayer that you hold on tight to Jesus until the day we meet face to face, no matter if you are sick or healed before that day.

A good friend of mine, Cathy, shared this story on Facebook. It is a good example of us being loved without cause:

As some of you may remember, I lost my cat "Puff" this year in a very tragic way - a companion I had for twenty years. So I didn't want another cat, I wanted a puppy, but my apartment won't allow dogs, so I prayed for months but just did not know what to do. Then the other day I prayed "Lord, I do not know even how to choose a kitten and I'm not sure if that is what I should do anyway." I then said "Lord if you want me to have a kitten or cat, maybe you could bring it to my door so I would know that it is the one. My last cat was not very affectionate and I do not want another one like that. I have been alone for many years and need some love but also I need to give love."

Two days later, I heard a kitten (actually close to one year old) right outside of my door late at night. You could tell she was a stray. This kind of thing does not just happen, as I have been in a season for a very long time, where my prayers seem to only go as far as the ceiling. Anyway, I thanked God for this little baby. I have had her for a few days now.

She is super-affectionate and she always wants me to hold her and she wants to be with me all the time. She just snuggles up right on my chest and looks up at me and stares at me. I have never had a pet like this one. She knows I have rescued her! Thank you

Lord for answered prayer and this sweet blessing! I want you to know that God cares about even the smallest details in our life. He perfects the things that concern us. (Psalm 138:8).

This is a heart-warming true story from a lady who suffers like us all.

Chapter 16
Heaven Will Be Glorious

"Let not your heart be troubled; you believe in God, believe also in Me. In My Father's house are many mansions; if it were not so, I would have told you. I go to prepare a place for you. And if I go and prepare a place for you, I will come again and receive you to Myself; that where I am, there you may be also." John 14:1-3.

I don't know about you, but there are many times when I ponder on my eternal home in Heaven. I long to live in a place that has no tears in it, because only good things are in Heaven! I so look forward to it, because sometimes, it's really hard to live on earth. Not that I have that many problems, it's just that time passes so slow some days and I look forward to all the wonderful activity that's waiting for me in my pro

To many who suffer, I sometimes feel that their heart has the same longing and anticipation for Heaven's glory. I have often talked to people about not wanting to be here anymore and they remind me of my purpose on earth. And that's true, I do have a purpose on earth that I need to complete. But that purpose doesn't stop me thinking about Heaven and the end to all suffering.

I have been privileged to actually see in visions parts of Heaven and so I know a little about it. I hope what I share here will give you the faith to continue on your journey and let you look forward with wonderful anticipation, to your final destination.

God has in mind a special job for everyone to do on earth and it is the type of work that you would love to do. But because of circumstances, many of us have had to shelve our dream. We live in a material world, so there are constant bills to pay on earth. Doing your dream job may not financially provide enough to cover your responsibilities. So in order to be responsible, many people have to settle for something more tedious and far less satisfying.

However, in Heaven, this will not be the case. In Heaven, you will discover that shelving dreams is a thing of the past. No longer will you work at a tedious job, you will be doing the thing that God originally put in your heart to do when He first created you. There are no bills to pay in Heaven, so that in itself is an enormous benefit. Therefore, every single adult will be given a totally satisfying work to do, which will be their dream job.

For example: If you always wanted to be an artist on earth, but you discovered that artwork sales were not sufficient to support your lifestyle or commitments, you had no choice but to do something less satisfying. But in Heaven, it's so different! There will be free art lessons that you can take; there will be other artists you can do life with; you will have your own studio in Heaven and people will come shopping and pick out your artworks for themselves or for other people they love.

Everything in Heaven is free! There is no corrupting influence at all in Heaven. You do work in Heaven but not for money, because money is useless. You will work because that is what you were born to do. Doing what you were born to do will bring you the most happiness. You will be able to go out with no money and shop to your heart's content.

People have loved ones who will soon be arriving, this cause much excitement. As someone who really knows these new arrivals, they can begin to furnish their homes in Heaven with special little love gifts according to their loved one's tastes. People in Heaven go out shopping as often as they do on earth and they collect things that bring them or others joy.

There are restaurants and cafes in Heaven and they are never overbooked. You can always seem to get a seat and you don't have to book in advance like you might have to on earth. You can eat at your favorite restaurant as often as your heart desires. There are cafes that serve coffee and other delightful drinks as well as an appetising menu. You will never tire of going out to enjoy yourselves.

Of course, in your house, you will have a kitchen and be able to cook if you love to cook, or else, you can just order the food and the food will just appear for you. Your house will be your dream home, a place that earth's money could never afford. I have seen my house in Heaven and its full of all the things that I like.

There are all sorts of sports in Heaven that people enjoy. Every person who wants to play any type of sports will have the ability to play and improve their game by receiving as much professional free coaching as they want to.

In Heaven, you will have the time to improve in your musical, theatrical, artistic creative ability or anything else that takes your fancy. You will make friends with like-minded people and your lessons will be free. People won't arrive in Heaven perfect at anything, except of course being holy and righteous, because God did that at their salvation.

There are colleges in Heaven where you can learn anything that you want to learn, however, there are no government debts in the form of student loans when you finish them. There is personal coaching and mentoring in Heaven to help you understand your course of study, and to make sure everyone who starts something gets to finish it - if they want to, of course.

Jesus spends time with everyone in Heaven, face to face in a very personal way. Not only do you get to worship Jesus and the Father in the throne room, you get to meet the Father and Jesus with one on one time. Jesus spoke in the book of Revelation that those who overcome will get to sit down on His throne. When you sit on Jesus' throne, you will be welcome to chat with the Father. God wants to give you all a big hug and wipe the tears of joy from your eyes.

Everyone will get plenty of time in the throne room to worship. Don't get worried that your job might take you away from your time with God. In Heaven, there is worship in the air and it is everywhere! The singing is glorious in Heaven. You will never be deprived of worship and time with God and Jesus.

For us who suffer, Heaven will be such a glorious place to be. Gone will be the pain and suffering. Gone will be the anxiety and the tears. In Heaven, we will be known and loved for who we are inside. There will be no more having to put on a brave face, for we will be set free and set free indeed!

What does the Word of God say about Heaven? Let's look at 1 Corinthians 2:9,

"Eye has not seen, nor ear heard,

Nor have entered into the heart of man.

The things which God has prepared

For those who love Him."

For a more extensive look at Heaven, see Kat Kerr's books, *Revealing Heaven 1 and 2*. I want to thank you personally for reading this book. I hope that it has encouraged you as I intended it to do.

Matthew Robert Payne

August 2015

I'd Love to Hear from You!

As an author, I regard the feedback of my readers highly. When considering a book, many people weigh reviews in the balance. If you enjoyed this book, please consider helping others to make an informed decision. Leaving a review on Amazon can help spread the message of the gospel, increase others' faith through these books, and be a great way to support this ministry for free!

I'd love to hear from you in one of these ways:

My Email survivors.sanctuary@gmail.com
My Website http://www.matthewrobrtpayneministries.net
My Facebook group
https://www.facebook.com/groups/OpenHeavensGroup/
You can donate to my ministry at http://personal-prophecy-today.com

How to Sponsor a Book Project

If you have been blessed by this book, you might consider sponsoring a book for me. It normally costs me between fifteen hundred and two thousand dollars or more to produce each book that I write, depending on the length of the book.

If you seek the Holy Spirit about financing a book for me, I know that the Lord would be eternally grateful to you. Consider how much this book has blessed you and then think of hundreds or even thousands of people who would be blessed by a book of mine. As you are probably aware, the vast majority of my books are ninety-nine cents on Kindle, which proves to you that book writing is indeed a ministry for me and not a money- making venture. I would be very happy if you supported me in this.

If you have any questions for me or if you want to know what projects I am currently working on that your money might finance, you can write to me at **survivors.sanctuary@gmail.com** and ask me for more information. I would be pleased to give you more details about my projects. You can sow any amount to my ministry by simply sending me money via the PayPal link at this address: http://personal-prophecy-today.com/support-my-ministry/ You can be sure that your support, no matter the amount, will be used for the publishing of helpful Christian books for people to read.

Other Books by Matthew Robert Payne

The Parables of Jesus Made Simple
The Prophetic Supernatural Experience
His Redeeming Love - A Memoir
Prophetic Evangelism Made Simple
Kingdom Nuggets: A Handbook for Christian Living
Great Cloud of Witnesses Speak
Your Identity in Christ
Writing and Self Publishing Christian Non Fiction

You can view more of my books on my author page at Amazon at http://tinyurl.com/m34snbb

www.ingramcontent.com/pod-product-compliance
Lightning Source LLC
Chambersburg PA
CBHW030332230426
43661CB00032B/1385/J